LEARNING WITH COLOUR
FASCINATING FACTS

A Treasury of Information on Hundreds of Subjects

By Bertha Morris Parker
Revised by Dr Heinz Woltereck
Illustrated by Lowell Hess

HAMLYN
LONDON · NEW YORK · SYDNEY · TORONTO

CONTENTS

ACKNOWLEDGEMENTS
Pages 16, 17, 21: All photographs Mt. Wilson and Palomar Observatories except Great Nebula in Orion by Clarence P. Custer, M.D.
Some of the illustrations in this book were done by Mel T. Crawford, Albertine Dependorf, James Gordon Irving, Harry McNaught, Gregory Orloff and Edelgard Pfisterer.

First published 1970
Third impression 1972
Published by The Hamlyn Publishing Group Limited
London · New York · Sydney · Toronto
Hamlyn House, Feltham, Middlesex, England
This Edition © Copyright The Hamlyn Publishing Group Limited 1970
© Copyright by Western Publishing Company, Inc., 1951, 1952, 1954, 1956, 1957, 1958, 1960, 1962. All rights reserved. © Copyright by
Delphin Verlag, Stuttgart and Zurich, 1966
ISBN 0 601 07937 X
Printed Offset Litho in England by Cox & Wyman Ltd
London, Fakenham and Reading

PYTHAGORAS

ANCIENT MAP OF NIPPUR

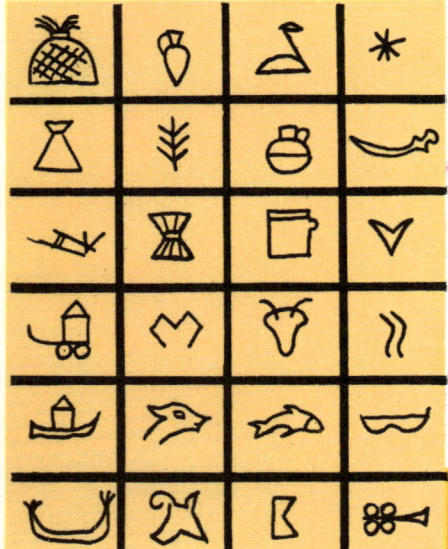

ANCIENT SUMERIAN SCRIPT

THE ROUTE OF THE 'VICTORIA'

SPHINX WITH THE HEAD OF QUEEN HATSHEPSUT

MONTGOLFIER BALLOON

FAMOUS FIRSTS

EQUATOR
24,902 miles

The earliest paintings we know about are the Lascaux cave paintings at Dordogne, France. These were painted about 65,000 B.C.

The oldest map in the world is an Egyptian map known as the Turin Papyrus, which is dated about 1320 B.C. It shows the plan of a gold mine.

The first written language known, the cuneiform script of the Sumerians, dates from about 4240 B.C.

Round about the same time, the Egyptians worked out the world's first solar calendar, with a year of 365 days.

The earliest doctor whose name has come down to us was an Egyptian, Imhotep, who is said to have lived as long ago as 2980 B.C.

The first known code of laws dates from about 2145 B.C. It is the code of Ur-Nammu, a third-dynasty king of Ur (the country now known as Syria). This collection of laws is about 200 years older than the famous code of Hammurabi.

The first recorded murder trial took place in Sumer about 1850 B.C. One archaeologist has called it 'The Case of the Silent Wife'.

The first 'farmer's almanac' was written in Sumer about 1700 B.C.

The first fully alphabetic script is believed to have been developed by the Semetic peoples, around 1500 B.C., although our own alphabet is based on the Greek system.

The first known manual on the care of horses was written in Sumerian some 3400 years ago. It was found in Turkey.

The first great woman recorded in history was Queen Hatshepsut of Egypt. Her reign was approximately from 1511–1480 B.C.

The earliest shipwrecked vessel to have its treasure found at the bottom of the sea (in 1960) was wrecked on an island off the coast of what is now Turkey about 1400 B.C.

The first Olympic Games of which there is a record were held in 776 B.C. just outside the small town of Olympia in Greece and consisted only of a foot race of about 200 yards. The first modern Olympic Games were held in Athens in 1896 with nine nations competing.

Pythagoras of Greece (582?–507 B.C.) was the first person to claim that the earth is round.

Democritus of Greece (460?–357? B.C.) was the first person to suggest that the Milky Way is composed of a vast number of faint stars.

Aristarchus of Samos (310?–230? B.C.) was the first person to state the belief that the earth travels around the sun and that the moon travels around the earth.

Eratosthenes (276–194 B.C.) was the first man to work out the circumference of the earth at the equator. He was such a good geographer and mathematician that his figures were only 238 miles off.

Ts'ai Lun of China was the first man to invent paper in 105 A.D.

Porcelain was first made in China during the 7th century.

In 1510, Peter Henlein of Nuremberg in Germany made the first pocket watch.

The first printed book we know about was made in China in 848 A.D. by Wang Chieh. He carved each page in a block of wood. Printing with movable type came considerably later, printing with porcelain type about 900 years ago in China, and printing with metal type some 500 years later in Germany.

The first mechanical clock was made in China in 725 A.D. by I'Hsing and Liang Ling-tsan.

The first ship to sail around the world was the Spanish ship *Victoria*. Commanded on the first half of the voyage by Ferdinand Magellan and, after his death, by Sebastian del Cano, the *Victoria* left Spain on 20 Sept. 1519, and did not return until 6 Sept. 1522.

The first microscope was invented by Zacharias Jansen about 1590.

In 1610 Johann Kepler of Germany invented the first astronomical telescope, and worked out the laws of planetary motion.

Roger Bacon of England (c. 1214–92) was the first known man to make use of lenses in a telescope, though it is believed that Arab scientists, living many years earlier, already knew something about the magnifying power of lenses.

The first lightning conductor was invented in 1752 by the American statesman and philosopher Benjamin Franklin.

The first successful balloon was designed by the Montgolfier brothers and was launched in France on 5 June 1783. The first manned flight was made in a similar balloon on 21 Nov. 1783.

In 1765 James Watt of Scotland invented the first steam engine.

André-Jacques Garnerin made the first parachute jump in Paris on 22 Oct. 1797, from a height of about 6,500 feet.

The English physician, Edward Jenner (1749–1823) was the first man to invent vaccination as a method of preventing small-pox.

Railed trucks were used for mining in Alsace as early as 1550, but in 1804, the Englishman Richard Trevithick built the first self-propelled locomotive. In 1829 George Stephenson built his famous *Rocket* from which all later versions of the steam engine were to derive.

The first successful steam-driven boat was the paddle-wheel steamer, the *Charlotte Dundas*. She was built in Scotland by William Symington (1763–1831) using an engine invented by James Watt as early as 1769.

The first photograph was taken by the Frenchman Joseph Niépce in 1826.

The English surgeon, Lord Lister (1827–1912), was the first man to introduce antiseptic methods into surgery by the use of chemicals.

The first sewing machine was invented by the Austrian tailor, Joseph Madersperger, in 1830.

In 1830, the Englishman, Michael Faraday, proved that an electric current could be generated in a loop of wire.

The first telegraph was invented by the American, Samuel B. Morse, who also invented the code (of dots and dashes) for transmitting messages, which is named after him.

The English engineer, Isambard Kingdom Brunel, (1806–1859), best-known for his innovations in bridge-building and railway construction, also designed and built the first transatlantic wooden paddle-steamer, the *Great Western*, in 1837; the first large iron-hulled screw steamer, the *Great Britain* in 1843; and the *Great Eastern*, in 1858, which was propelled by both paddles and screw, had the first double iron hull and was the prototype of the modern ocean liner.

In 1845, R. W. Thomson of England invented the first pneumatic tyre.

The first successful electric light bulb was invented by Heinrich Goebel of Germany in 1854.

The first car fitted with an internal combustion engine was made by Siegfried Marcus of Austria in 1875; it was, however, soon superseded by Karl Benz's Motorwagen in late 1885.

The first telephone system, invented by two Americans, Gay and Bell, went into production in 1876.

The first successful gramophone was built by Thomas Alva Edison in the United States in 1878.

The first electric railway was designed by Werner von Siemens and was opened at the Berlin Trades' Exhibition on 31 May 1879. It was the Berlin electric tramway, 300 yards long.

The earliest bicycle powered by an internal combustion engine was built in 1885 by Gottlieb Daimler of Germany. It was the prototype of the motor-cycle.

The first building to be called a skyscraper, the Home Insurance Company building in Chicago, was built in 1885.

The discovery of X-rays was first made in 1895 by Professor Wilhelm Konrad Röntgen of Germany.

'The Yellow Kid' by Richard Outcault was the first coloured cartoon. It appeared in 1895 in the *New York World*.

In 1895 the Italian, Guglielmo Marconi, made the first long-distance (1 mile) transmission of signals by wireless telegraphy.

In 1898 Pierre and Marie Curie of France were the first scientists to discover radium.

Orville Wright made the first successful flight in an aeroplane at Kitty Hawk, North Carolina, U.S.A., on 17 Dec. 1903.

In 1905 Albert Einstein (1879–1955) published his theory of relativity. According to this theory light always travels with the same speed relative to an observer, however fast he moves in relation to anything else. In these days of space exploration, Einstein's theory is of immense importance.

The North Pole was first reached by Commodore Robert E. Peary and his party of five on 6 April 1909.

The South Pole was first reached on 14 Dec. 1911 by the Norwegian, Roald Amundsen.

In 1911, Lord Rutherford (1871–1937) from New Zealand, announced his nuclear theory of the atom and in 1918 succeeded in splitting the atom for the first time.

The first public demonstration of television was given by John Logie Baird of Scotland on 26 Jan. 1926.

In 1927, the American aviator, Charles Lindbergh, was

Commander William R. Anderson of the United States Navy achieved the first submarine trans-polar crossing in the atomic-powered *Nautilus*, in 1958.

the first man to fly across the Atlantic in an aeroplane.

The first television broadcasting station in the world was opened on 2 Nov. 1936 at the Alexandra Palace, London.

On 2 Dec. 1942, the first controlled nuclear chain reaction was achieved by Enrico Fermi at the University of Chicago, U.S.A.

The highest point on earth, the top of Mount Everest, was first reached on 29 May 1953 by Sir Edmund Hillary and the Sherpa, Tensing Norkhay.

On 6 May 1954, Roger Bannister of England became the first man to run a mile in less than 4 minutes. His time was 3 min., 59.4 sec.

The *Nautilus,* launched 21 Jan. 1954, at Groton, Connecticut, U.S.A., was the first atomic submarine. The first atomic merchant ship, the *N.S. Savannah* was launched 21 July 1959, at Camden, New Jersey, U.S.A. 'N.S.' stands for 'Nuclear Ship'.

The first man-made earth satellite, *Sputnik I,* was launched by the Russians on 4 Oct. 1957.

The world's first atomic power station for producing electricity for civilian use began operation in 17 Oct. 1956, at Calder Hill in England.

The first non-stop, round-the-world jet plane flight was completed on 18 Jan. 1957, by three United States Air Force bombers under the command of Major General Archie J. Old. The flight took 45 hours and 19 minutes.

The first crossing of the Antarctic continent was made in 1958 by Dr Vivian Fuchs with a party of twelve men. The journey was made from Shackleton base to Scott base via the South Pole and took 99 days, ending on 2 Mar. 1958.

The first artificial planet, or satellite, *Lunik I,* was shot into space on 2 Jan. 1959.

On 23 Jan. 1960, Dr Jacques Piccard and Lt Donald Walsh, U.S. Navy, became the first men to travel 6.78 miles down into the ocean. This descent took place in the Challenger Deep off the Marianas Trench in the Pacific Ocean and was made in the bathyscaphe *Trieste.* The descent took 4 hours, 48 minutes.

The first successful manned space flight was made by Flight Major Yuri Gagarin on 12 April 1961. He completed a single orbit of the Earth in the U.S.S.R. space ship *Vostok I.*

On 16 June 1963, Jnr Lt (now Flight Major) Valentina Tereshkova completed 48 orbits of the Earth in *Vostok VI* and became the first woman to be launched into space.

The first man to leave a space-ship during orbit was Lt-Col Aleksey Leonov who, on 18 March 1965, spent 20 minutes outside the satellite *Voskhod II,* attached to it only by a 16-foot line.

The first time man ever set foot on the moon was 21 July 1969, when Neil Armstrong, commander of Apollo 11, stepped down on to the moon's surface from the lunar module *Eagle.* Armstrong hailed this first step as 'one small step for a man, one giant leap for mankind'.

The above illustration of a photograph taken from the Apollo 8 spacecraft shows a close-up of the moon's surface with the earth, partly cast into shadow, in the distance. Inset, the Apollo 8 command module in which Colonel Frank Borman, Captain James Lovell and Major William Anders made the six-day, half-million mile trip to the moon and back over Christmas, 1968. At the start of the journey, after two orbits of the earth, Apollo 8 headed for the moon at a speed of 24,200 m.p.h. It orbited the moon ten times in 20 hours at a minimum height of 60 miles before returning to earth.

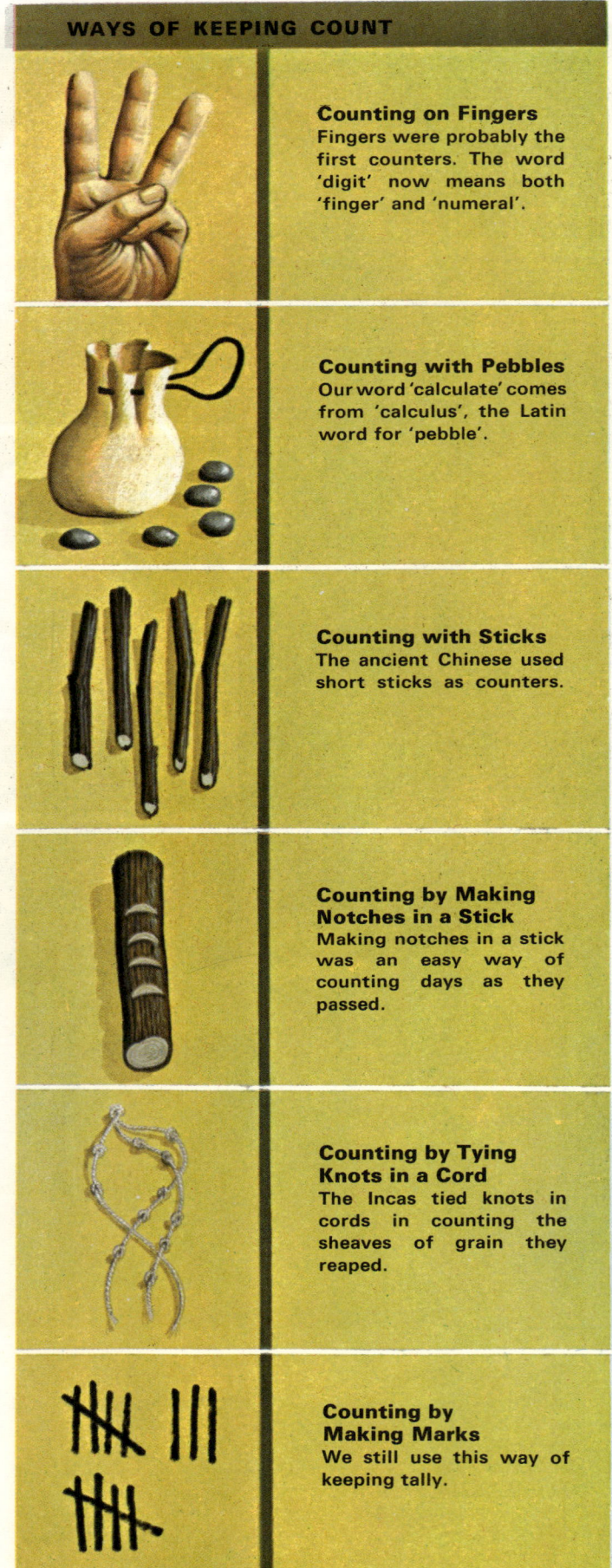

Counting on Fingers
Fingers were probably the first counters. The word 'digit' now means both 'finger' and 'numeral'.

Counting with Pebbles
Our word 'calculate' comes from 'calculus', the Latin word for 'pebble'.

Counting with Sticks
The ancient Chinese used short sticks as counters.

Counting by Making Notches in a Stick
Making notches in a stick was an easy way of counting days as they passed.

Counting by Tying Knots in a Cord
The Incas tied knots in cords in counting the sheaves of grain they reaped.

Counting by Making Marks
We still use this way of keeping tally.

WAYS OF CALCULATING

CHINESE ABACUS

With an abacus a person works out a problem by moving beads on wires. Each bead has a value. On the first wire at the right, each bead below the crossbar stands for 1, each bead above for 5. The beads on the second wire stand for 10's below and 50's above, on the third wire for 100's and 500's, and so on.

$$\begin{array}{r} .89 \\ .25 \\ 1.07 \\ \hline 2.21 \end{array}$$

NUMERALS

Calculating with numerals is now, in a great many parts of the world, much more common than calculating with an abacus. Five hundred years ago calculating with numerals was often called 'calculating with the pen' to contrast it with calculating with beads or some other counters.

CALCULATING MACHINES

Today there are calculating machines that can add, subtract, multiply and divide very, very rapidly. Some are simple; others are very complicated. A big electronic computer can solve in a few hours a problem that would take a person working with pencil and paper several hundred years to solve.

NUMERALS

EGYPTIAN
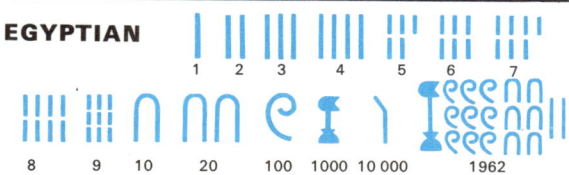

BABYLONIAN
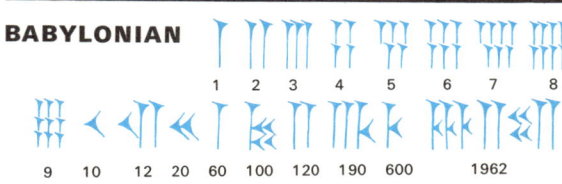

GREEK
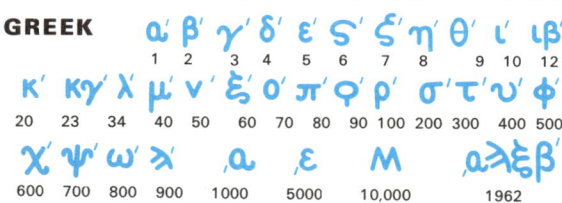

ROMAN
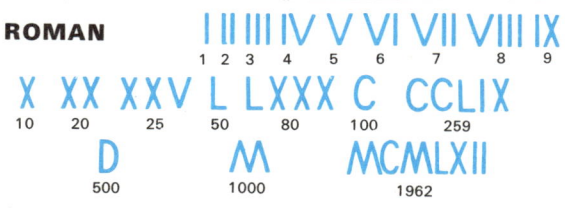

CHINESE

MAYA
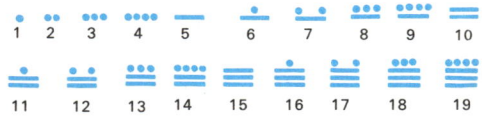

HINDU

ARABIC

In the number system followed in Great Britain, a million is a thousand thousands, a billion is a million millions, and so on as follows, each a million times the one before:

Trillion	Nonillion	Quindecillion
Quadrillion	Decillion	Sexdecillion
Quintillion	Undecillion	Septendecillion
Sextillion	Duodecillion	Octodecillion
Septillion	Tredecillion	Novemdecillion
Octillion	Quattuordecillion	Vigintillion, or

1,000,000,000,000,000,000,000,000,
000,000,000,000,000,000,000,
000,000,000,000,000,000,000

THE ANCIENT EGYPTIAN WAY OF MULTIPLYING AND DIVIDING

The ancient Egyptians added and subtracted just as we do, using their own numerals, of course, but they multiplied and divided by a process of doubling. Let us suppose they wished to multiply 40 by 13. They doubled and redoubled the multiplicand thus:

There would be no point in doubling another time, for the number in the first column would then be 16, which is greater than the multiplier. They then picked out the numbers in the first column which added up to 13 and added the corresponding numbers in the second column to get the product:

```
1- 40
2- 80
4-160
8-320
```

```
1- 40
4-160
8-320
13-520
```

These are the steps in dividing 520 by 13:

```
 1- 13
 2- 26
 4- 52
*8-104*
16-208
*32-416*
40-520*
```

13

MEASURES OF LENGTH

CUBIT
The people of long ago used parts of their own bodies in measuring. The cubit was the length of the forearm. The cubit is often mentioned in the Bible.

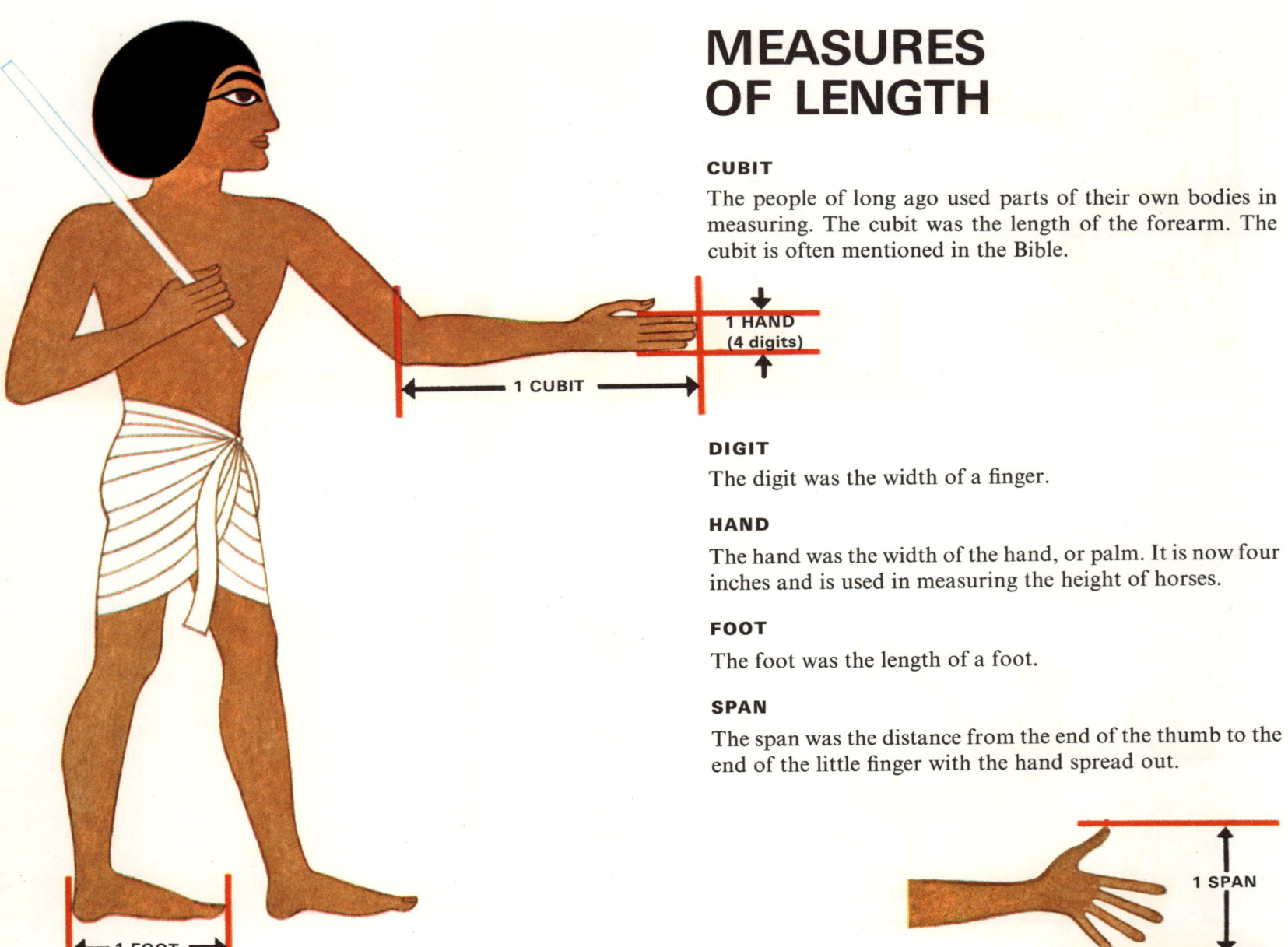

DIGIT
The digit was the width of a finger.

HAND
The hand was the width of the hand, or palm. It is now four inches and is used in measuring the height of horses.

FOOT
The foot was the length of a foot.

SPAN
The span was the distance from the end of the thumb to the end of the little finger with the hand spread out.

MEASURES OF LENGTH (English System)

12 inches	=1 foot
3 feet	=1 yard
5½ yards (16½ feet)	=1 rod
40 rods	=1 furlong
8 furlongs (1760 yards or 5280 feet)	=1 mile

COMPARISONS:

1 inch	= 2.54 centimetres
1 foot	= 0.3048 metres
1 yard	= 0.9144 metres
1 mile	= 1.6093 kilometres
1 centimetre	= 0.3937 inches
1 metre	= 3.2808 feet
1 kilometre	= 0.62137 mile

MEASURES OF LENGTH (metric system)

10 millimetres	=1 centimetre
10 centimetres	=1 decimetre
10 decimetres (100 centimetres or 1000 millimetres)	=1 metre
1000 metres	=1 kilometre

NAUTICAL MEASURES (English system)

6 feet	=1 fathom
100 fathoms	=1 cable's length
10 cable lengths	=1 nautical mile

COMPARISONS:

1 nautical mile	=1.15157 miles
1 nautical mile	=1853.2 metres

1 YARD

FURLONG

'Furlong' is short for 'furrow long.' A farmer could plough a furrow just so long before he needed to let his oxen rest a while.

INCH

In the beginning the inch was the width of the thumb. In the 14th century, Edward II of England decreed that an inch was to be three barleycorns (grains of barley) laid end to end.

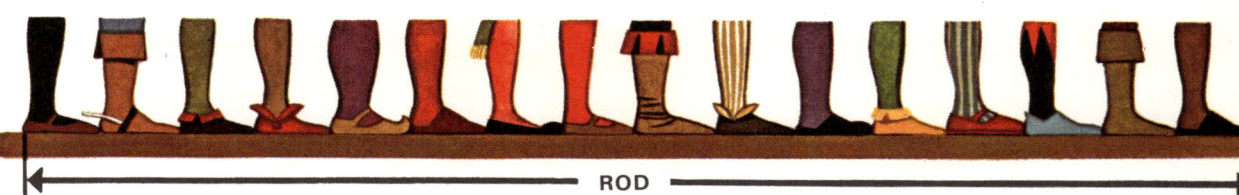

ROD

YARD

In the 12th century, Henry I of England decreed that the yard was to be the distance from the end of his nose to the end of his thumb.

ROD

In the 16th century, the length of the rod was set by having sixteen men, as they were coming out of church, put their left feet one behind the other.

MILE

The word 'mile' is short for *mille passuum,* the Latin words for '1,000 paces.'

PACE

A pace was a double step.

MEASURES OF AREA

ACRE

Four furrows, a furlong long and an oxgang apart (the width of a team of eight oxen), was the measure of the first acre.

TABLES OF AREA

MEASURES OF AREA (English system)
144 square inches	= 1 square foot
9 square feet	= 1 square yard
$30\frac{1}{4}$ square yards	= 1 square rod
160 square rods	= 1 acre
640 acres	= 1 square mile

MEASURES OF AREA (metric system)
100 square millimetres	= 1 square centimetre
100 square centimetres	= 1 square decimetre
100 square decimetres	= 1 square metre
100 square metres	= 1 are
100 ares	= 1 hectare
100 hectares	= 1 square kilometre

COMPARISONS:
1 acre	= 40.4687 ares
1 square mile	= 259 hectares
1 hectare	= 2.471 acres
1 square kilometre	= 0.3861 square miles

MEASURES OF WEIGHT

STONE

The Babylonians used polished stones as weights. They used different stones for weighing different things. Today in the United Kingdom, a 'stone' equals 14 pounds.

GRAIN

One grain of wheat is very much like another. The ancient Greeks and Egyptians used grains of wheat as weights. The 'grain' of today thus had its beginning long ago.

SHEKEL

The Babylonians, Hebrews, and other people of the Near East had coins called shekels. The name came from the name of a Babylonian unit of weight.

CARAT

The Arabs used the seeds of the carob tree as weights. The 'carat' now used in weighing diamonds began as a 'carob seed.'

POUND

The story of the pound begins with the Greeks. The word comes from a word for 'weight.' The abbreviation (lb) comes from *libra*, the Latin word for pound.

OUNCE

The Romans divided their pound into 12 *unciae*. The *uncia* became our ounce, but there are 16 ounces in a pound when common materials are weighed.

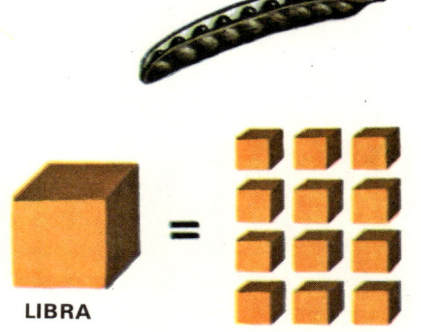

LIBRA = UNCIAE

ENGLISH SYSTEM
Troy Weight
(Jewels, precious metals)

24 grains	= 1 pennyweight
20 pennyweights	= 1 ounce
1 ounce	= 480 grains
12 ounces	= 1 pound

AVOIRDUPOIS WEIGHT
(Ordinary commodities)

16 drams	= 1 ounce
16 ounces	= 1 pound
7000 grains	= 1 pound
14 pounds	= 1 stone
2000 pounds	= 1 short ton
2240 pounds	= 1 ton (20 hundredweight)

APOTHECARIES' WEIGHT
(Drugs)

20 grains	= 1 scruple
3 scruples	= 1 drachm
8 drachms	= 1 ounce
12 ounces	= 1 pound

COMPARISONS:

1 ounce (avoirdupois)	= 28.3495 grams
1 pound (avoirdupois)	= 453.39 grams
1 ton	= 1016 kilograms or 1.016 metric tons
1 gram	= 15.432 grains
1 kilogram	= 2.2046 pounds (avoirdupois)
1 metric ton	= 2204.6 pounds (avoirdupois)

METRIC SYSTEM

10 milligrams	= 1 centigram
100 centigrams	= 1 gram
100 grams	= 1 kilogram
1000 kilograms	= 1 metric ton

NOTE: The Apothecaries' ounce is the same as the Troy ounce, but the Apothecaries' *drachm* is not the same as the Avoirdupois *dram*. A fluid *drachm* is equal in weight to *two* Avoirdupois *drams*.

Gill

Pint

Quart

Gallon

MEASURES OF CAPACITY

GALLON, QUART, PINT, GILL

The name 'gallon' is supposed to have come from an old French word for 'bowl.' 'Quart' is short for 'quarter gallon.' (There came to be a slightly different quart for measuring dry materials.) The name 'pint' comes from the *painted* mark on old vessels for measuring. 'Gill,' strangely, comes from an old word for 'tub.'

HANDFUL

The handful was a common measure of capacity among very primitive peoples. When English pilgrims first landed in America, they found that Red Indians measured corn by the handful.

HEAP

The heap has also been a common measure among primitive peoples. Of course, the heap is not at all an accurate measure.

GOURDFUL

North American and South American Indians measured liquids by the gourdful. Because gourds vary in size and capacity, they are not very accurate measures either.

HOGSHEAD

In England in 1423 the hogshead was made a standard measure for measuring liquids. It gets its name from a kind of cask or barrel called a hogshead.

ENGLISH SYSTEM
Dry Measure

2 pints	= 1 quart
8 quarts	= 1 peck
4 pecks	= 1 bushel
8 bushels	= 1 quarter

Liquid Measure

4 gills	= 1 pint
2 pints	= 1 quart
4 quarts	= 1 gallon
1 gallon	= 160 fluid ounces

Apothecaries' Fluid Measure

60 minims (*min.*)	= 1 fluid drachm
8 fluid drachms	= 1 fluid ounce
16 (U.S.) fluid ounces	= 1 pint
20 (U.K.) fluid ounces	= 1 Imperial pint
8 pints	= 1 gallon
8 Imperial pints	= 1 Imperial gallon

METRIC SYSTEM

10 millilitres	= 1 centilitre
10 centilitres	= 1 decilitre
10 decilitres	= 1 litre
10 litres	= 1 decalitre
10 decalitres	= 1 hectolitre
10 hectolitres	= 1 kilolitre

COMPARISONS:

1 bushel	= 36.37 litres
1 quart	= 1.136 litres
1 centilitre	= .352 fluid ounces
1 litre	= .880 quarts
1 hectolitre	= 2.749 bushels or 21.997 gallons

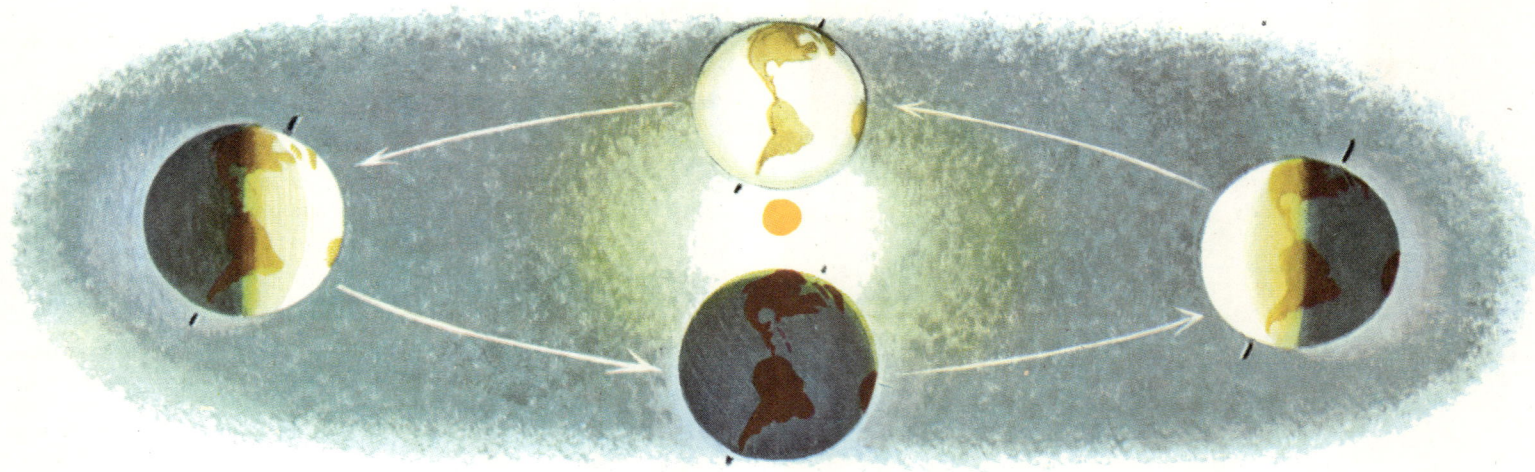

TERMS USED IN ASTRONOMY

APHELION. The earth's orbit is not a perfect circle. The point at which it is farthest from the sun is the aphelion.

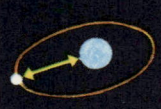

APOGEE. The point in its orbit at which the moon, or any satellite is farthest from the earth, or the central point of its orbit, is the apogee.

ASTEROIDS. Asteroids are very tiny planets. They are sometimes called planetoids. Most asteroids have orbits between the orbits of Mars and Jupiter.

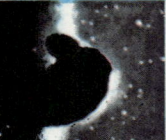

DARK NEBULA. A dark nebula is a vast cloud of star dust and gas not close enough to any stars to be lighted up by them. A famous dark nebula is the Horsehead Nebula.

ECLIPSE. An eclipse occurs when one heavenly body gets wholly or partly into the shadow of another.

GALAXY. A galaxy is a vast group of stars. Our sun is in the galaxy called the Milky Way. A galaxy is sometimes called a star city or an island universe.

YEAR. A sidereal year is the length of time it takes a planet to travel around the sun once. The earth's sidereal year is 365 days, 6 hours, 9 minutes, and 10 seconds long. Our calendar year is not quite the same, partly because it would be inconvenient for a year to end in the middle of a day.

COMET. The word 'comet' comes from 'coma,' the Latin word for 'hair.' A comet gets its name from the tail of gas and dust that streams out from it as it approaches the sun.

CONJUNCTION. When two heavenly bodies are in the same direction as viewed from the earth, we say that they are in conjunction.

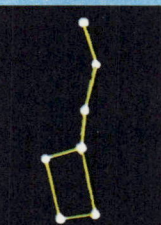

CONSTELLATION. The word 'constellation' means 'stars together.' Originally a constellation was simply a group of stars which seem to be close together as viewed from the earth. To astronomers, now, a constellation is a section of the heavens named for the chief group of stars in it. There are 88 constellations.

METEOR. Meteors are small bodies, many no larger than a grain of sand, which travel around the sun. Every day millions enter the earth's atmosphere. As they fall through the air they become white-hot and are called shooting stars or, if bright enough, fire-balls or bolides.

METEORITE. Most meteors that enter the earth's atmosphere turn to vapour before they reach the earth's surface. Those that do fall upon the earth are called meteorites.

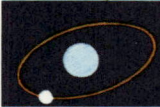

MOON. A moon is a heavenly body which travels around a planet. The earth has only one moon while Jupiter has twelve. Moons are natural satellites.

NEBULA. A nebula is a great cloud of gas and star dust far out in space. A nebula glows like a distant star if it is lighted up by light from a star.

NOVA. A nova is a star which has exploded so that it is thousands or millions of times as bright as before. 'Nova' is a Latin word meaning 'new.' But a nova is not really new. It is merely newly bright. Novae usually fade rather quickly.

OPPOSITION. When another planet or the moon is exactly opposite the sun as viewed from the earth, it is said to be in opposition.

PERIGEE. The point in its orbit at which the moon, or any satellite comes closest to the earth, or the central point of its orbit, is the perigree.

PERIHELION. The point in its orbit at which the earth is nearest the sun is the perihelion.

PLANET. A planet is a globe which travels around the sun and which gives off no light of its own. The earth is a planet.

ROTATE. A body rotates by turning on its own axis. The earth rotates on an axis which joins the north pole to the south pole.

SATELLITE. 'Satellite' is another word for 'moon.' A number of artificial satellites have been launched as a way of studying space and as a way of transmitting signals from country to country.

SUN. The star we call the sun is the centre of our Solar System.

SOLAR SYSTEM. The Solar System consists of the sun and of all the planets, moons, asteroids, comets and meteors which travel around it.

SPIRAL. A galaxy which looks, through a telescope, like the one in the picture is called a spiral. Sometimes it is called a spiral nebula. This name came into use before astronomers knew that the great whirls they saw were vast groups of stars rather than clouds of glowing gas.

STAR. A star is a glowing globe that shines by its own light. Another word for 'star' is 'sun.' When people talk about the stars they usually mean all suns except our own sun.

STAR CLUSTER. A star cluster is a group of stars. There are about a hundred known star clusters in our own galaxy, amongst which there are a variety of globular clusters.

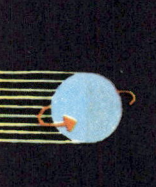

DAY. A sidereal (or star) day is the time it takes a moon or a planet to turn around once on its axis. A solar day is the average time from noon (when the sun is highest in the sky for the day) to noon. The earth's solar day, because the earth travels around the sun, is about 4 minutes longer than its sidereal day. Our calendar is based on the solar day. The sidereal days in a year number one more than the solar days.

REVOLVE. To revolve is to travel around another body. The earth revolves around the sun.

ORBIT. The path a heavenly body follows in travelling around another heavenly body is called an orbit. The word 'orbit' comes from the Latin word meaning 'circle,' but few if any orbits are perfect circles.

UNIVERSE. The universe includes all the millions and millions of galaxies and the space between.

ZENITH. The zenith is the point in the sky directly above a person standing on earth. The zenith differs on all parts of the globe.

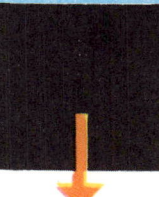

ZODIAC. The zodiac is made up of the constellations along the path which the sun appears to follow in the course of a year. Because of the journey of the earth around the sun, the sun appears to be in first one constellation and then another.

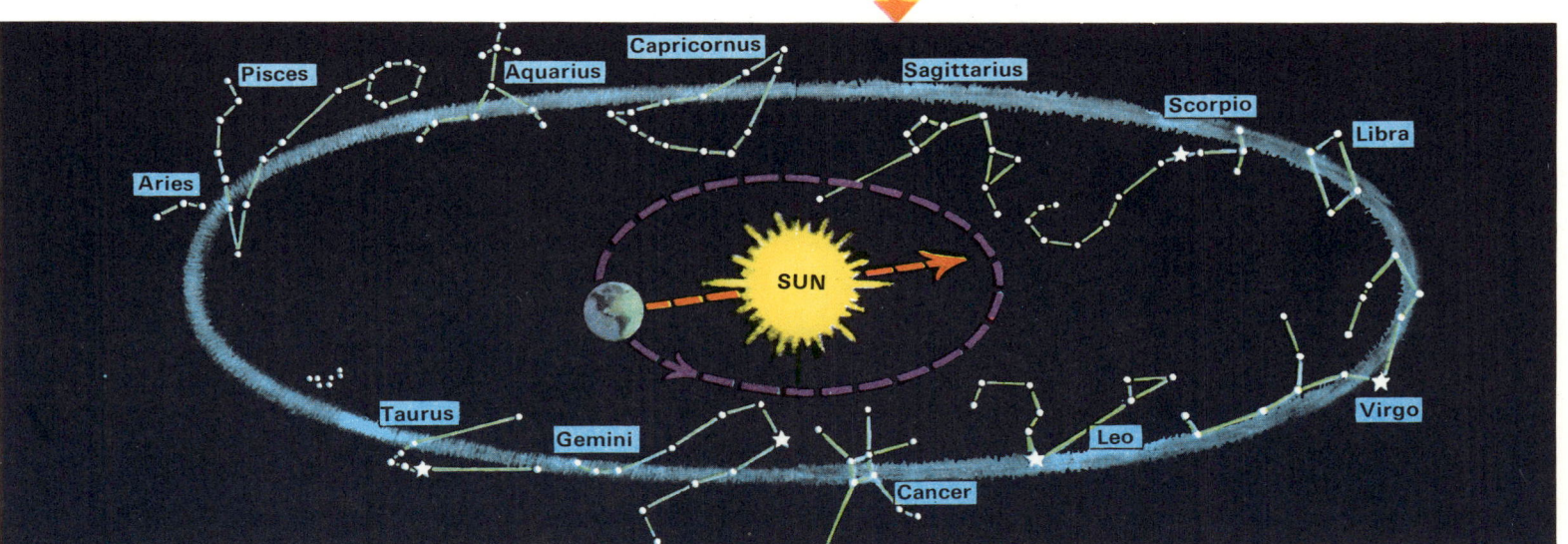

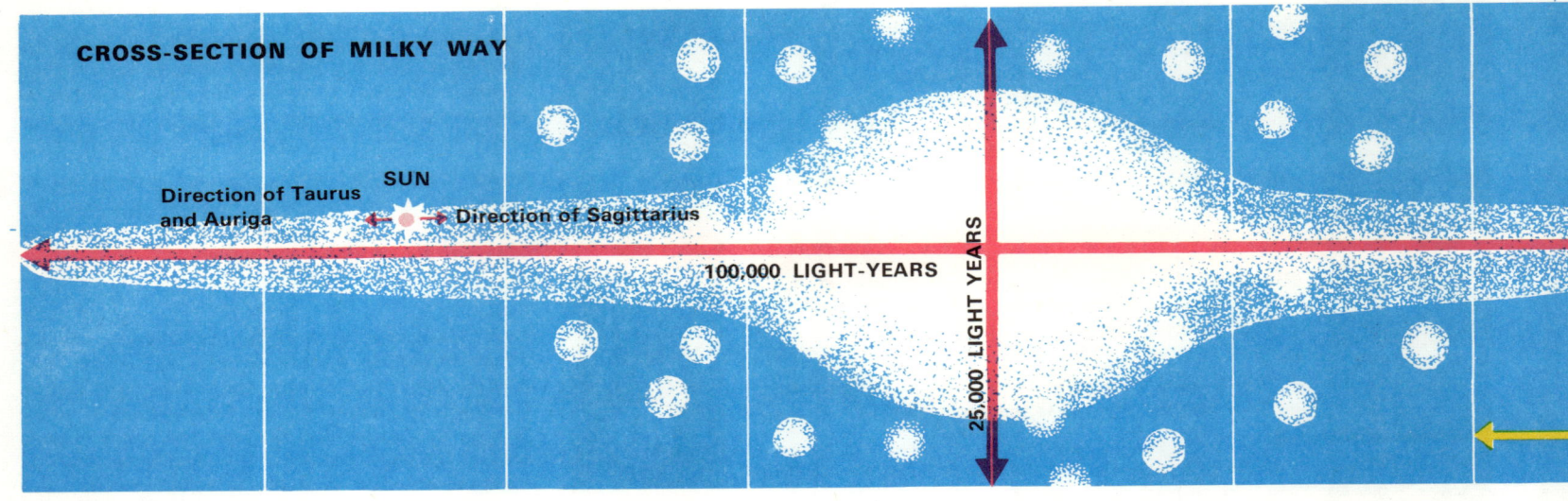

CROSS-SECTION OF MILKY WAY

Direction of Taurus and Auriga

SUN

Direction of Sagittarius

100,000 LIGHT-YEARS

25,000 LIGHT YEARS

This diagram shows the shape of the Milky Way and where the sun is placed within it.

ASTRONOMICAL NUMBERS

As the earth whirls on its axis, a spot on the equator moves just over 1,000 miles an hour.

The earth travels about 1,100 miles a minute (18½ miles a second) in its journey around the sun. In a day it travels more than 1½ million miles.

Strangely enough, the diameter of the earth's orbit is almost exactly 1,000 times the distance that light travels in one second.

The earth's yearly journey around the sun is nearly 600 million miles. Every ten-year-old has travelled nearly six thousand million miles even if he has never been away from home.

The sun and its planets move about 170 miles a second as the Milky Way galaxy whirls around. Even so it takes the sun some 200 million years to make one swing around the centre of the galaxy.

The galaxies in the universe are rushing away from one another. Some are travelling as fast as 70,000 miles a second.

It would take more than one million earths to make a ball as large as the sun.

Some of the great 'flames' that shoot up from the sun (solar prominences) are hundreds of thousands of miles high. The record height is 1,050,000 miles.

It would take 27 thousand million suns to make a ball as large as the giant red star Epislon Aurigae.

About one million meteors reach our atmosphere every hour. All but a very, very few turn to vapour before they reach the earth's surface. But in space travel, meteors can be a real danger.

There are at least 100 thousand million stars in our Milky Way galaxy.

There are known to be more than a thousand million galaxies in the universe. There may be even more.

If all the stars in the Milky Way galaxy had names, it would take 4,000 years to say all their names if they could be said one every second without stopping.

In all the galaxies together there are probably as many stars as there are grains of sand on all the world's sea-shores.

Our sun's nearest star neighbour is about 25 million million miles away.

In spite of all the billions of stars, space is not crowded. It is no more crowded with stars than North America would be with chipmunks if there were only three of them scampering about over the entire continent.

The distance across our Milky Way galaxy is about 100,000 light-years (100,000 times 6 million million miles).

Our sun is about 30,000 light-years (30,000 times 6 million million miles) from the centre of the Milky Way galaxy.

The Great Spiral in Andromeda is the nearest galaxy shaped like our Milky Way. It is more than 2 million light-years away (2 million times 6 million million miles).

The farthest galaxies our telescopes show are about 4 thousand million light-years away.

The temperature on the surface of the sun is 11,000°F. In the interior it is 30 million degrees.

In a year the sun uses up 22 million billion tons of its hydrogen in producing the energy it gives off. But even so it has enough to last for thousands of millions of years to come.

The Crab Nebula is a great cloud of gas that stretched for 17,700 thousand million miles. For more than 5,000 years it

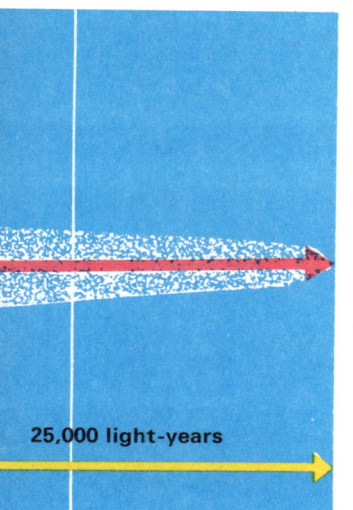

25,000 light-years

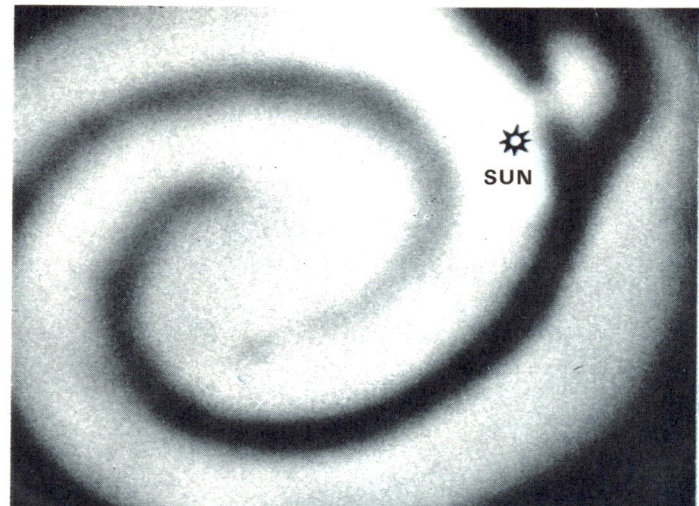

SUN

Our Milky Way galaxy as it would look viewed from another angle.

has been spreading out at the rate of 684 miles a second.

A tablespoonful of the material from a white dwarf star would weigh a ton or more if it could be brought to the earth.

Gravity on the surface of the white dwarf Companion of Sirius is 250,000 times as great as gravity on the earth's surface.

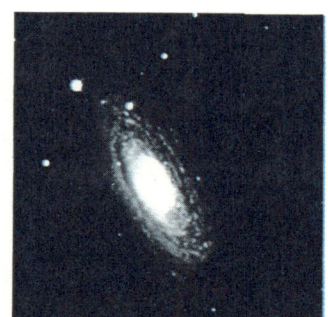

Galaxies are not all shaped like our Milky Way. But all galaxies are great 'star cities' made up of vast numbers of stars. Sometimes they are called 'island universes.'

STAR MAGNITUDES (BRIGHTNESS)

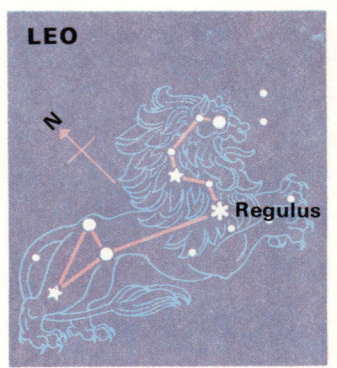

LEO

Regulus

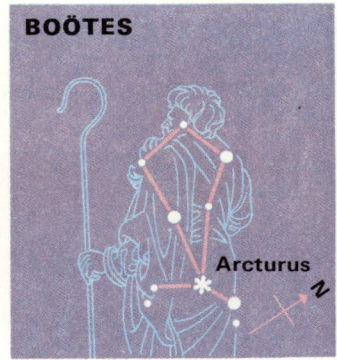

BOÖTES

Arcturus

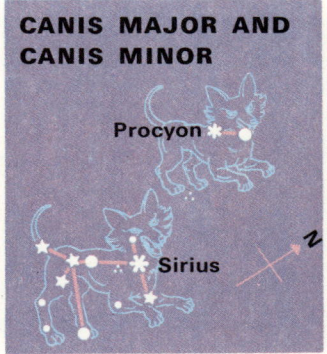

CANIS MAJOR AND CANIS MINOR

Procyon

Sirius

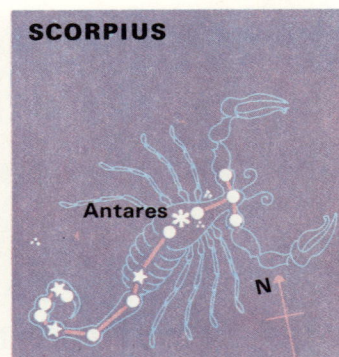

SCORPIUS

Antares

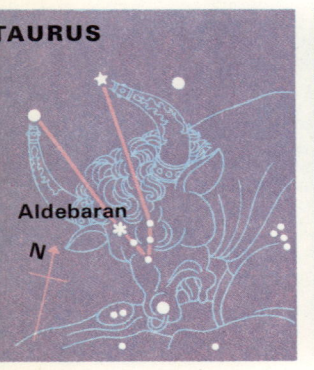

TAURUS

Aldebaran

N

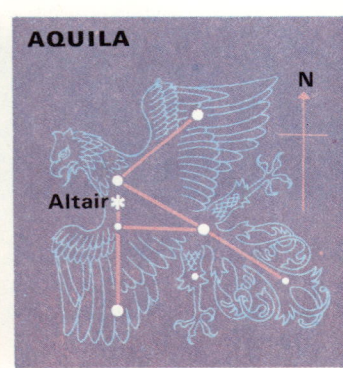

AQUILA

N

Altair

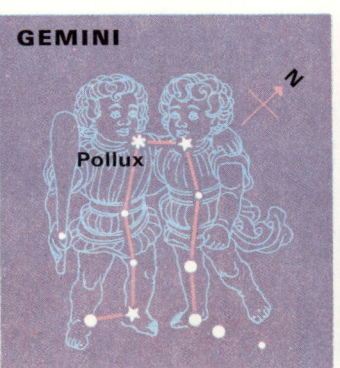

GEMINI

N

Pollux

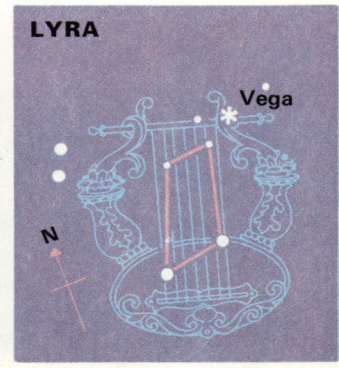

LYRA

Vega

N

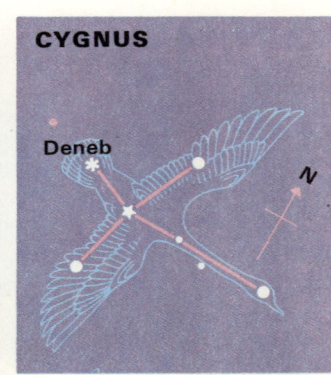

CYGNUS

Deneb

N

CONSTELLATIONS CONTAINING FOURTEEN OF THE TWENTY-ONE BRIGHTEST STARS

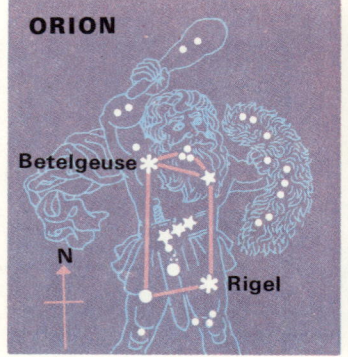

ORION

Betelgeuse

Rigel

N

VIRGO

N

Spica

You will notice that Auriga contains the bright star Capella and that Orion has two bright stars, Betelgeuse and Rigel.

22

Stars are grouped into magnitudes according to their brightness as seen from the earth. How bright a star looks in a moonless, cloudless night sky depends on how much light it gives off and how far away it is.

First-magnitude stars are, on the average, 2½ times as bright as second-magnitude stars; second-magnitude stars are 2½ times as bright as third-magnitude stars; and so on. First-magnitude stars are about 100 times as bright as sixth-magnitude stars. Without binoculars or a telescope, no one can see stars fainter than magnitude 6.

The magnitudes of the few very brightest stars are—1 or brighter (some have a zero or even minus reading).

On star maps different symbols are used for stars of different magnitudes. There are a number of different symbols used in constellation maps, of which one group is shown below.

✳ 1st magnitude or brighter ● 3rd magnitude
★ 2nd magnitude • 4th or 5th magnitude

 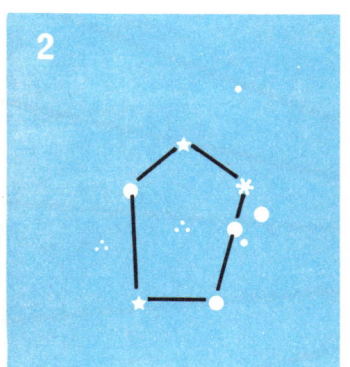 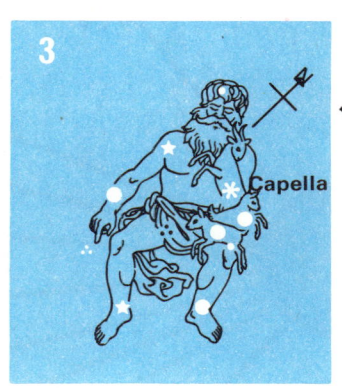

AURIGA
1. The stars of Auriga.
2. Auriga as it is usually shown on star maps.
3. To people of long ago, Auriga appeared as a charioteer with young goats on his lap.

THE TWENTY-ONE BRIGHTEST STARS IN ORDER OF THEIR BRIGHTNESS		
Star	**Distance in Light-years**	**Constellation**
Sirius	9	Canis Major (The Great Dog)
Canopus	163	Carina (The Keel of the Ship)
Alpha Centauri	4	Centaurus (The Centaur)
Vega	26	Lyra (The Lyre)
Capella	45	Auriga (The Charioteer)
Arcturus	32	Boötes (The Herdsman)
Rigel	900	Orion (The Hunter)
Procyon	10	Canis Minor (The Little Dog)
Achernar	67	Eridanus (The River)
Beta Centauri	90	Centaurus (The Centaur)
Altair	16	Aquila (The Eagle)
Betelgeuse	600	Orion (The Hunter)
Alpha Crucis	210	Crux (The Southern Cross)
Aldebaran	68	Taurus (The Bull)
Pollux	35	Gemini (The Twins)
Spica	230	Virgo (The Virgin)
Antares	410	Scorpius (The Scorpion)
Fomalhaut	24	Piscis Austrinus (The Southern Fish)
Deneb	408	Cygnus (The Swan)
Beta Crucis	490	Crux (The Southern Cross)
Regulus	79	Leo (The Lion)

SKY DISTANCES

UNITS OF MEASUREMENT USED BY ASTRONOMERS

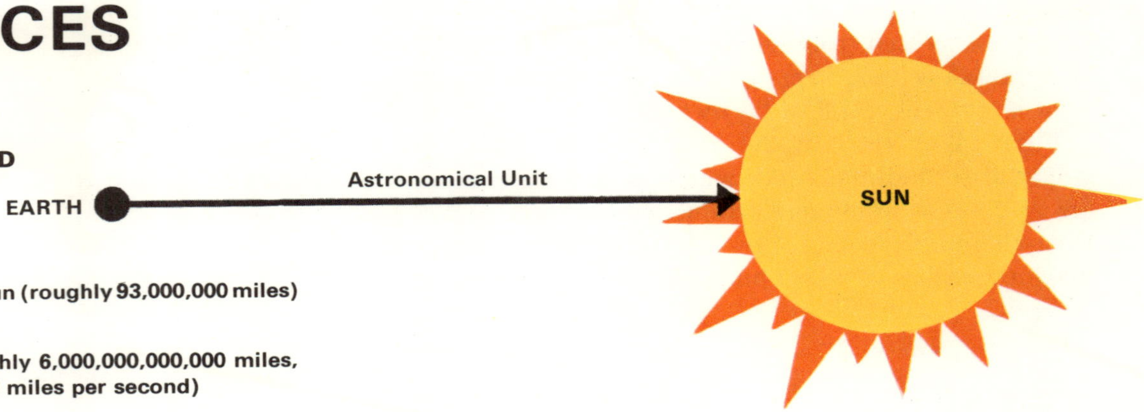

EARTH — Astronomical Unit → SUN

ASTRONOMICAL UNIT:
Average distance from the earth to the sun (roughly 93,000,000 miles)

LIGHT-YEAR:
Distance light travels in one year (roughly 6,000,000,000,000 miles, since light travels at the rate of 186,272 miles per second)

PARSEC:
3.26 light-years (roughly 19,000,000,000,000 miles)

ALPHA CENTAURI

ARCTURUS

4.3 LIGHT-YEARS

36 LIGHT-YEARS

34,000 LIGHT-YEARS

120,000,000 LIGHT-YEARS

4,100 LIGHT-YEARS

1,000 LIGHT-YEARS

2,300,000 LIGHT-YEARS

The little scenes suggest what was happening on the earth when the light that reaches our eyes tonight left these heavenly bodies. It takes light from the sun eight minutes to reach us.

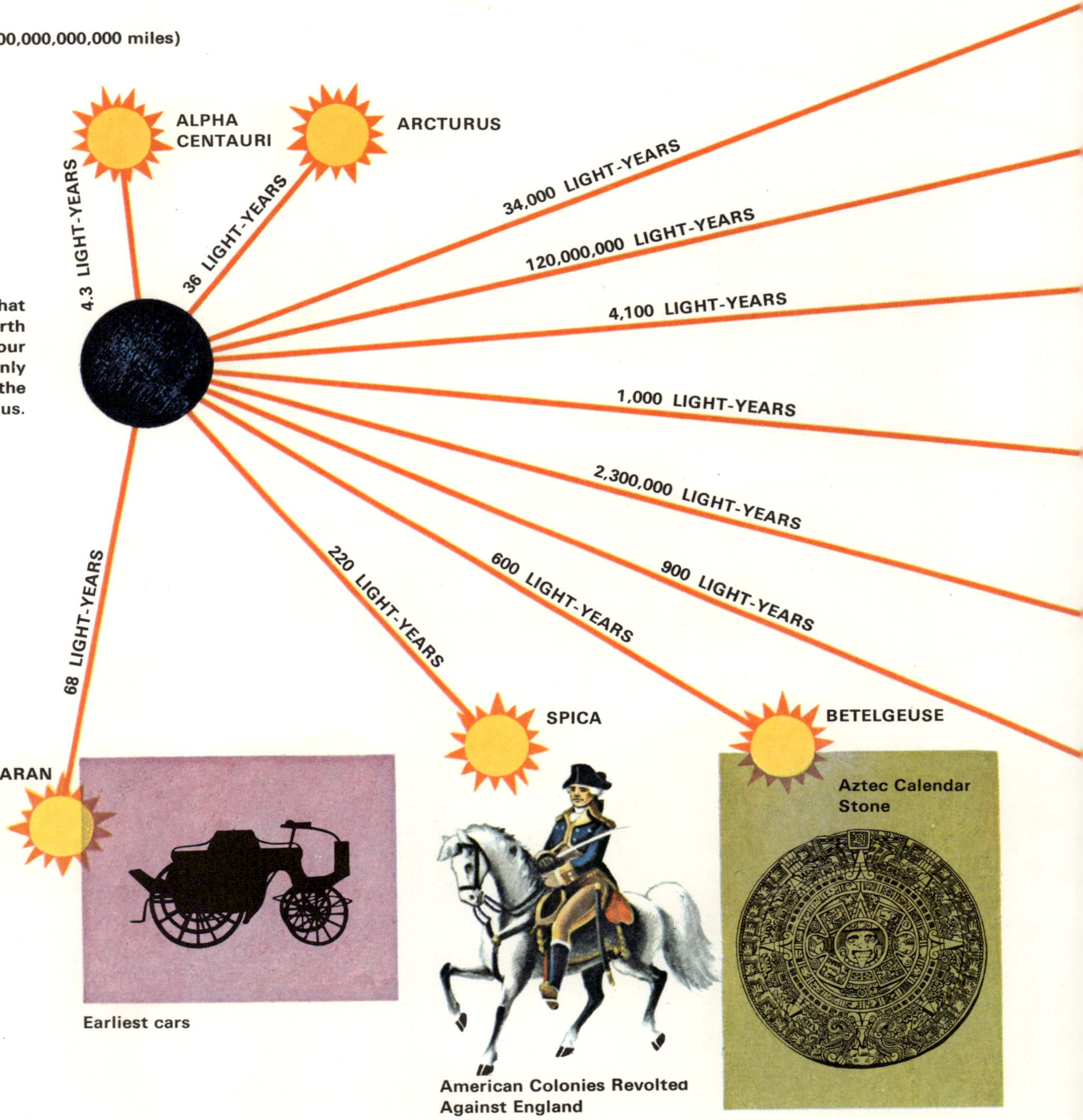

68 LIGHT-YEARS

220 LIGHT-YEARS

600 LIGHT-YEARS

900 LIGHT-YEARS

SPICA

BETELGEUSE

ALDEBARAN

Earliest cars

American Colonies Revolted Against England

Aztec Calendar Stone

Ice Age

Dinosaurs

GLOBULAR CLUSTER
IN HERCULES

GROUP OF NEBULAE
IN CORONA BOREALIS

Ancient
Egypt

CRAB NEBULA

GREAT NEBULA IN ORION

Vikings

RIGEL

GREAT NEBULA IN ANDROMEDA

Sabretooth
tiger

Norman Conquest

25

MERCURY

VENUS

EARTH

MARS

JUPITER

SATURN

URANUS

NEPTUNE

PLUTO

THE SUN

The sun is a yellow star. The sun is 864,000 miles in diameter; if it were hollow, there would be room inside it for 1,300,000 earths. It is 700 times as large as all its planets, moons, asteroids, comets and meteors put together.

The sun weighs 330,000 times as much as the earth.

A boy who weighs 7 stone, 2 lb on the earth would weigh $1\frac{1}{4}$ tons at the surface of the sun.

The temperature at the centre of the sun is about 30,000,000°F. The temperature at the surface is about 11,000°F. Strangely enough, the temperature in the corona is about 1,000,000°F.

The tongues of glowing gas called prominences often shoot up more than 100,000 miles from the surface.

Sunspots are great storms on the surface of the sun. A big sunspot could swallow up dozens of earths. The largest sunspot appeared in April 1947, and measured 7,000 million square miles.

The temperature in a sunspot is some 3,000 degrees lower than at other places on the sun's surface.

Sunspots occur in approximate eleven-year cycles: for 5 or 6 years the number gradually increases and then for 5 or 6 years they diminish. There have been periods when there have been very few. These periods are called 'quiet sun years.' One such period occurred in 1957–8.

The sun rotates on its axis, but some parts rotate faster than others. The period of rotation is about 25 days at the equator, and about 33 days at the poles. Such a difference is possible because the sun is not solid.

A great many of the chemical elements found here on earth are known to exist in the sun, but 95% of the sun's material consists of hydrogen and helium.

In one twenty-four hour period (one day), the sun will be about 345 thousand million tons lighter. For every second 564 million tons of hydrogen is changed into only 560 million tons of helium. The sun, therefore, loses about 4 million tons a second.

Although its hydrogen is being used up at a terrific rate, the sun has enough left to last for billions of years.

The earth gets less than $\frac{1}{2,000,000,000}$ of the energy the sun sends out.

If the people of Europe had to pay for the energy they get from the sun at the same rate that they pay for electricity from power plants, the yearly bill would be more than a thousand billion pounds.

If the sun died out and no longer gave us light and heat, all the earth's stores of coal, petroleum and other fuels could keep the earth as warm as it is now for only three days.

Solar batteries can now convert the energy of the sun's rays directly into a usable electric current.

26

THE ORBITS OF THE NINE PLANETS

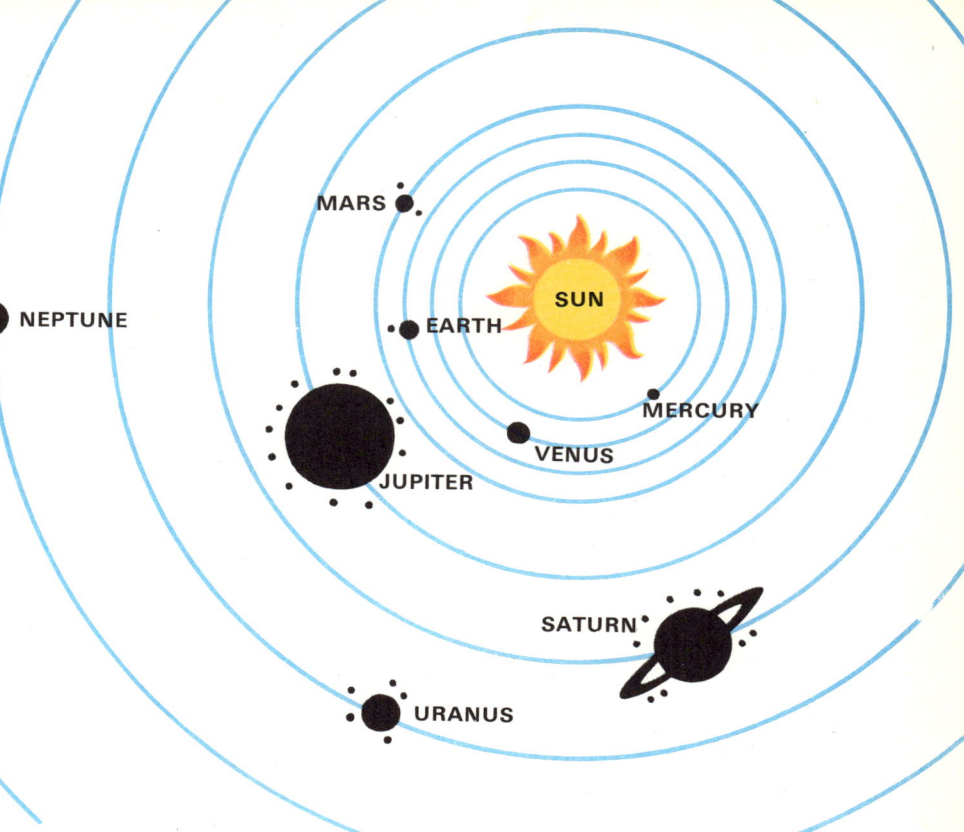

This chart shows the order of the orbits of the nine planets in our Solar System. It does not show the comparative distances of these orbits from the sun. In a book the planets and their orbits cannot be drawn to the same scale if the planets are made large enough to be seen. Actually, most of the Solar System is empty space. If, in making a model of the Solar System, a beach ball thirty inches across was used for the sun, a radish seed would be about the right size for Pluto. And, if the same scale used in choosing the models were used in placing them, the radish seed for Pluto would have to be put nearly two miles from the beach ball representing the sun.

PLANET STATISTICS

Planet	Symbol	Average Distance from the Sun in Millions of Miles	Diameter in Miles	Length of Time for Revolution Round the Sun	Length of Time for Rotation on Axis	Number of Known Moons
Mercury	☿	36	3,000	88 days	59 days	0
Venus	♀	67	7,600	243 days	243 days*	0
Earth	⊕	93	7,927	365¼ days	23 hr. 56 min.	1
Mars	♂	142	4,200	687 days	24 hr. 37 min.	2
Jupiter	♃	483	87,000	12 years	9 hr. 50 min.	12
Saturn	♄	886	75,100	29½ years	10 hr. 2 min.	10
Uranus	♅	1,783	30,900	84 years	10 hr. 48 min.	5
Neptune	♆	2,793	33,000	165 years	15 hr. 48 min.	2
Pluto	♇	3,666	3,500	248 years	6½ days (?)	0
Sun	☉		864,000		25 days 9 hr.	

*Radar techniques have established that Venus rotates clockwise, whereas other planets rotate counterclockwise.

BRIGHTNESS OF THE PLANETS

The planets all vary in brightness because, as a result of their travels around the sun, they are at varying distances from the earth.

MERCURY at its brightest is brighter than Sirius, the Dog Star, the brightest true star. It is, however, almost always hidden by the glare of the sun.

VENUS is the brightest of all the planets—much brighter than the Dog Star. Venus is so bright that it can sometimes be seen in the daytime.

MARS at its brightest is brighter than Mercury but not so bright as Venus. It looks like a reddish star.

JUPITER always looks like a bright yellowish star. At their brightest, Jupiter and Mars are about equally bright. At their palest, Jupiter is much brighter than Mars.

SATURN at its brightest is brighter than all the true stars except Sirius and Canopus. It is not, however, nearly so bright as Mars, Jupiter, Mercury and Venus at their brightest.

URANUS cannot be seen with the naked eye.

NEPTUNE can be seen only with a powerful telescope.

PLUTO is very faint and extremely hard to locate even with a 12-inch telescope.

COULD PEOPLE LIVE ON ANY OTHER PLANETS IN OUR SOLAR SYSTEM?

To be a possible home for people, a planet must have a fairly mild temperature, at least in some areas; a solid surface, at least in part; an atmosphere containing oxygen, but no poisonous gases; water; green plants to furnish food and sunlight.

The chart below shows whether, so far as scientists know, any of the other planets in the Solar System meet the requirements for sustaining human life.

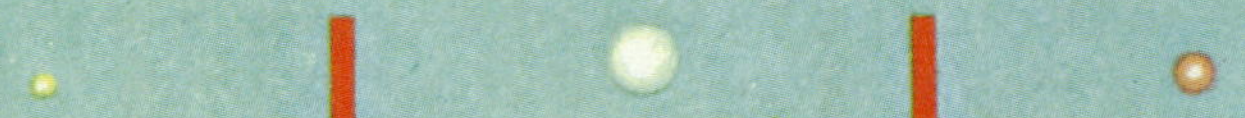

	MERCURY	VENUS	MARS
TEMPERATURE	 One half always very hot (about 650°F.); the other half always extremely cold (about —450°F.)	Hot. Surface protected somewhat by thick clouds. Surface temperature probably reaches 536°F.	Great extremes: in summer temperature may reach more than 100°F. in daytime and fall to far below 0°F. at night. Winters very cold.
WATER	 No evidence.	Probably some, but amount is not known. Heavy clouds may be formed by dust and water vapour.	Some, but not a great amount.
ATMOSPHERE	Little, if any, atmosphere.	Dense atmosphere, containing a great deal of carbon dioxide. No evidence of oxygen.	Very thin atmosphere, made up mostly of nitrogen and argon. Small amounts of carbon dioxide and probably of oxygen present.
GREEN PLANTS	 No evidence.	Possibly a very low form of plant life does exist.	Some very simple living things are thought to be present. Perhaps plants somewhat like lichens.
SOLID SURFACE	 Yes.	Solid surface is probably covered with a very dusty desert.	Yes.
SUNLIGHT	 Intense sunlight on one side; none on the other.	Yes, but very little can shine through the heavy clouds to the planet's surface.	Yes.
ANSWER	NO.	NO.	NO.

JUPITER	SATURN	URANUS	NEPTUNE	PLUTO
Extremely cold. Average temperature about —200°F.	Extremely cold. Average temperature about —225°F.	Extremely cold. Average temperature about —300°F.	Extremely cold. Average temperature about —325°F.	Extremely cold. Average temperature about —350°F.
Frozen, if any is present at all.	Rings made partly of ice crystals.	No evidence	No evidence.	No evidence.
Dense atmosphere made up chiefly of hydrogen, marsh gas, and ammonia, all poisonous or suffocating.	Atmosphere much like Jupiter's.	Not known.	Not known.	Not known.
No.	No.	No.	No.	No.
Surface perhaps liquid. Planet may, however, be surrounded by a shell of ice.	Probably only innermost core solid. May, however, be surrounded by a thick shell of ice.	Not known.	Not known.	Not known.
Yes, but too weak to have much heating effect.	Yes, but too weak to have much heating effect.	Yes, but very weak.	Yes, but very weak.	Yes, but much more like our moonlight than our sunlight.
NO.	NO.	NO.	NO.	NO.

TIDES

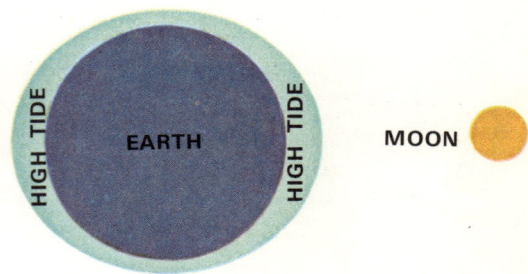

High tides occur on opposite sides of the earth at the same time. The moon pulls up the water on the part of the earth nearest it. On the opposite side of the earth, where the pull is least, the water bulges away from the moon.

High tides are much higher along certain coasts than along others. The highest tides known occur in the Bay of Fundy, between Nova Scotia and New Brunswick. Sometimes the high tide is 70 feet higher than the low tide there.

High tides come at different times each day because of the travelling of the moon around the earth.

High tides are on the average 12 hours and 25 minutes apart.

The sun also causes tides, but the moon is so much closer to the earth that the tides it causes are much more noticeable. But when the sun, earth and moon are in a straight line—at the new moon and at the full moon—the sun and moon are causing tides in the same place at the same time and the tides are higher than usual. These extra-high tides are called spring tides. When the moon is at first quarter or last quarter, the sun and moon are pulling at right angles to each other and we have tides less high than usual—these are called neap tides.

AT FULL MOON

AT NEW MOON

LUNAR ECLIPSES

An eclipse of the moon is called a lunar eclipse.

There cannot be a lunar eclipse unless the moon is full.

A lunar eclipse can be seen everywhere on the side of the earth facing the moon.

When the moon is wholly in the earth's shadow, the eclipse is called total.

Even when the moon is wholly in the earth's shadow, it does not always disappear. It looks dull red because the earth's atmosphere bends red rays so that they strike it.

In any one spot, a total eclipse lasts for about 2 hours.

A partial eclipse occurs when the moon passes through the edge of the earth's shadow.

There are never more than three lunar eclipses in a year, and there may be none.

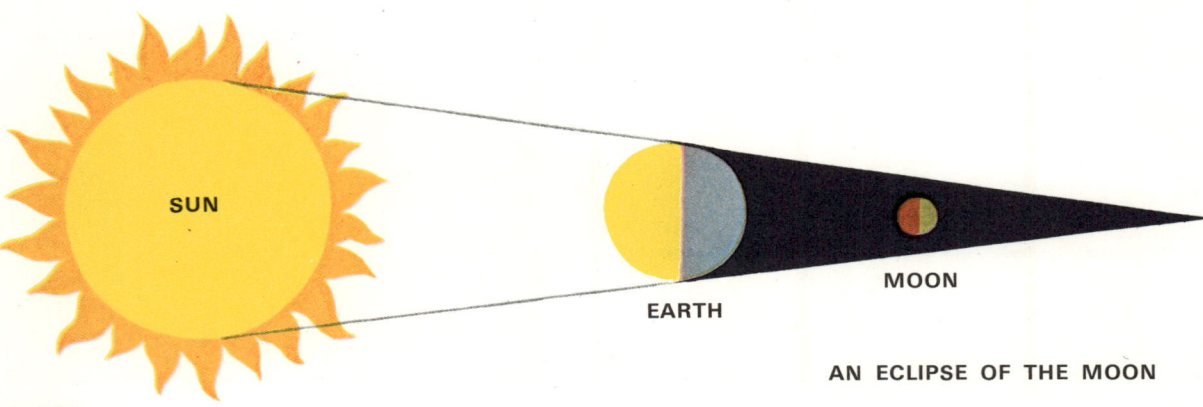

AN ECLIPSE OF THE MOON

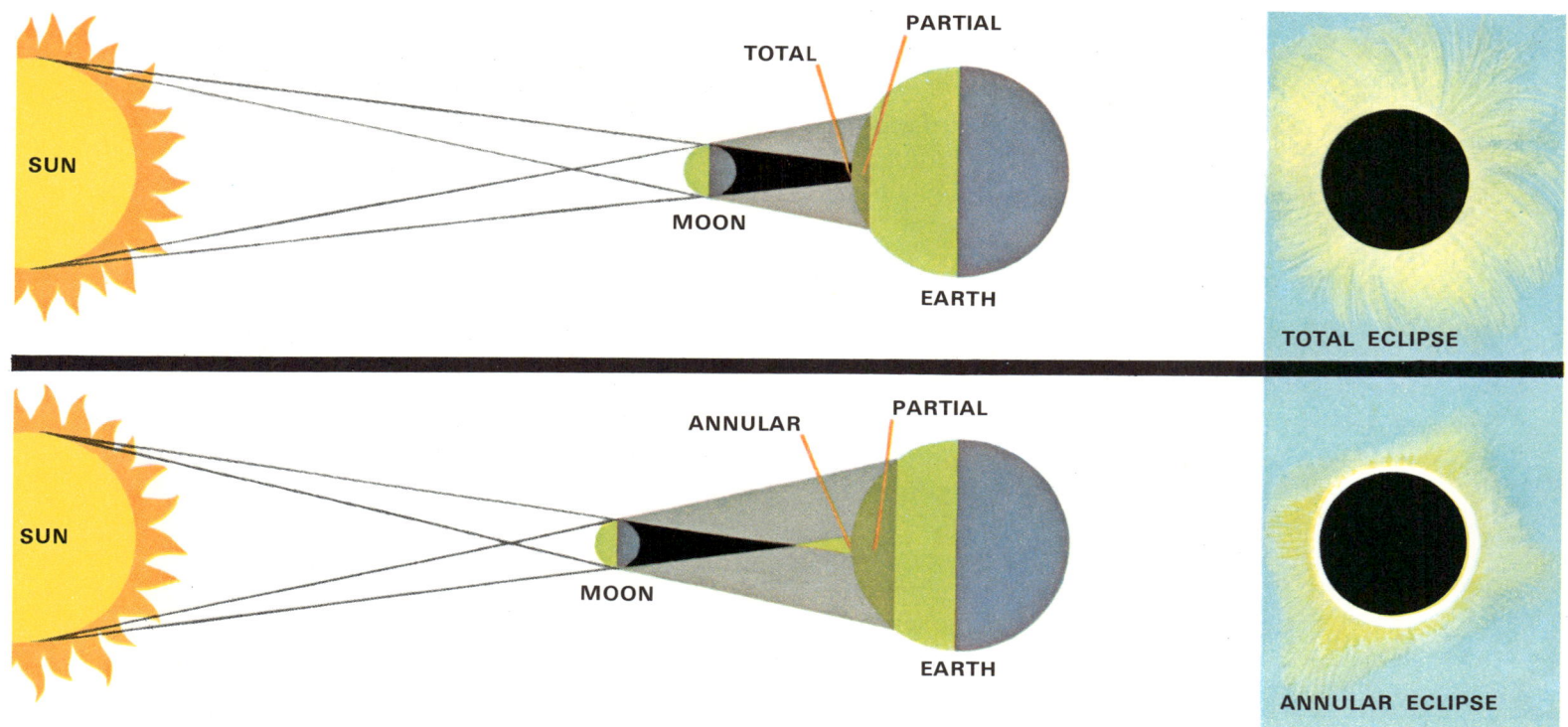

SOLAR ECLIPSES

An eclipse of the sun is called a solar eclipse.

There cannot be an eclipse of the sun except at the time of the new moon.

If the view of the total disc of the sun is shut off by the moon, we say that the eclipse is total. If the view of all the disc except a narrow rim around the edge is shut off, we say that the eclipse is annular. All other eclipses are partial.

Of all solar eclipses only about 28 % are total.

During a total eclipse the sun's corona comes into view.

When the moon hides the sun from part of the earth, that part of the earth is really in the moon's shadow. The path of an eclipse is the path of the moon's shadow.

There are normally at least two solar eclipses in a year, and there may be five.

A total solar eclipse never lasts more than eight minutes in one place. Its path is only about 100 miles wide.

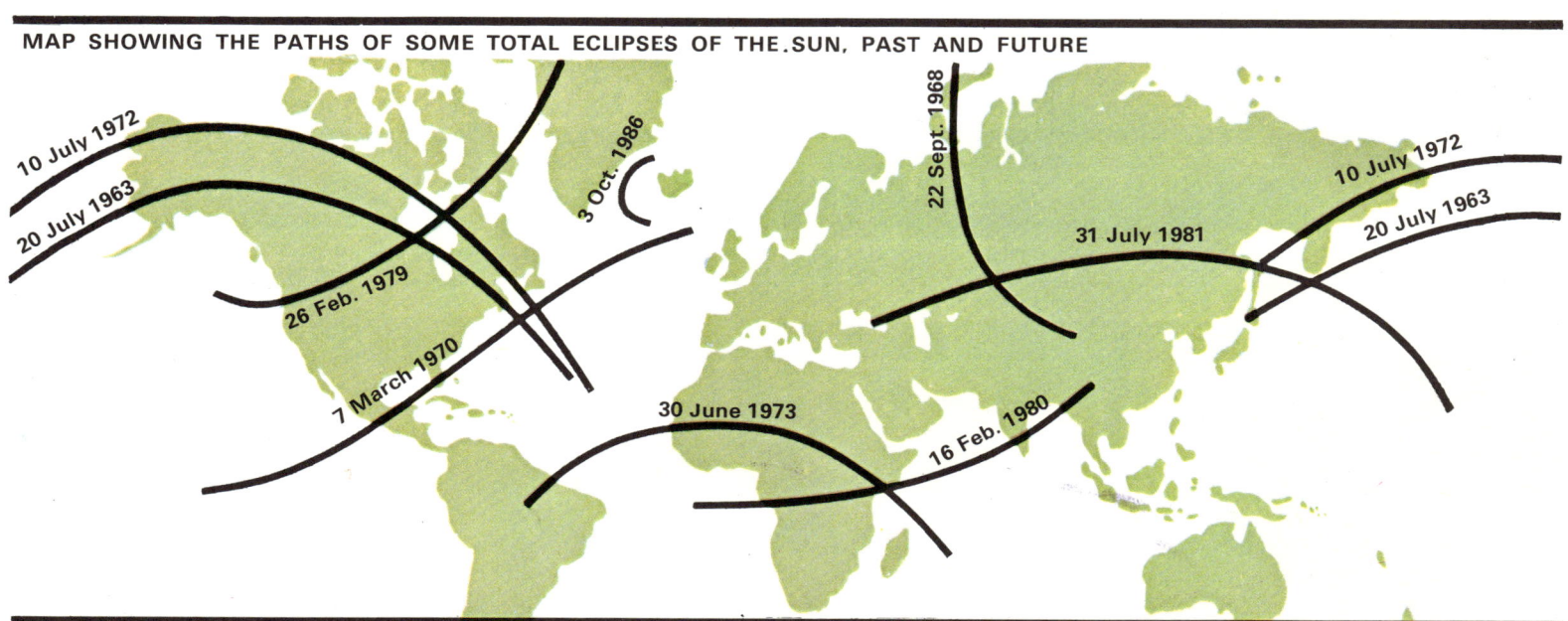

MAP SHOWING THE PATHS OF SOME TOTAL ECLIPSES OF THE SUN, PAST AND FUTURE

SATELLITES

The earth has one satellite, or moon. Five of the other planets have moons. Some of their moons are larger than the earth's moon, but none as big as the earth's moon in proportion to the planet it travels around. As the table above shows, most of the moons in the Solar System are a great deal smaller than the earth's moon.

How big a moon would look from the surface of the planet it travels around depends not only on the moon's size but also on how far away it is from the planet. Phobos, the larger of the two moons of Mars, would look about a third as big as our moon even though our moon is more than 200 times as big. Phobos is only 3,700 miles from the surface of Mars while our moon is, on the average, 239,000 miles from the surface of the earth. Jupiter's largest moons are more than 650,000 miles from the surface of Jupiter.

Moons differ greatly in the length of time it takes them to circle their planets. Phobos needs only 7 hours and 39 minutes to circle Mars, while Jupiter IX needs 758 days for its journey around Jupiter. The moon circles the earth in about $27\frac{1}{3}$ days.

Planet *	Satellite	Year of Discovery	Estimated Diameter in Miles
Earth	Moon	?	2160
Mars	Deimos	1877	5
	Phobos	1877	8
Jupiter	Io (I)	1610	2000
	Europa (II)	1610	1800
	Ganymede (III)	1610	3100
	Callisto (IV)	1610	2800
	Amalthea (V)	1892	120
	VI	1904	62
	VII	1905	20
	VIII	1908	12
	IX	1914	12
	X	1938	12
	XI	1938	12
	XII	1951	12
Saturn	Titan	1655	3000
	Iapetus	1671	680
	Rhea	1672	800
	Dione	1684	600
	Tethys	1684	600
	Mimas	1789	300
	Enceladus	1789	380
	Hyperion	1848	300
	Phoebe	1898	120
	Janus	1967	?
Uranus	Titania	1787	680
	Oberon	1787	620
	Ariel	1851	500
	Umbriel	1851	370
	Miranda	1948	180
Neptune	Triton	1846	2200
	Nereid	1949	180

* Mercury, Venus and Pluto do not have any natural satellites, as far as we know.

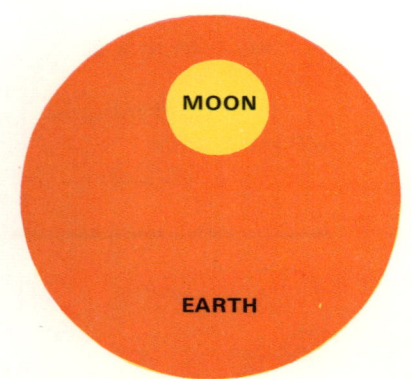

Scale: 1 in. = 4,000 mi.

HOW THE EARTH AND ITS MOON COMPARE IN SIZE

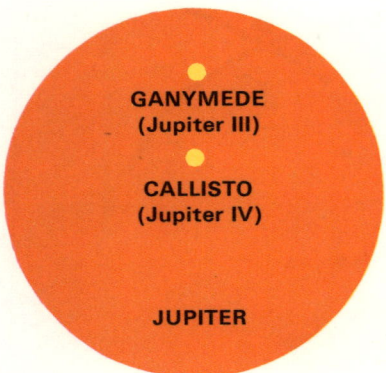

Scale: 1 in. = 45,000 mi.

HOW JUPITER AND ITS LARGEST MOONS COMPARE IN SIZE

ARTIFICIAL SATELLITES

Artificial or man-made satellites were first suggested by Sir Isaac Newton in his book on 'Mathematical Principles of Natural Philosophy,' which was first published in 1687. But it was not until 4 October 1957 that a real artificial satellite was put into orbit. This was *Sputnik I* which was designed under the direction of Dr Sergey Pavlovich Korolyov (1906–1966) of the U.S.S.R. *Sputnik I* is believed to have had a life of 92 days; it weighed 184.3 lb and had a diameter of 22.8 inches.

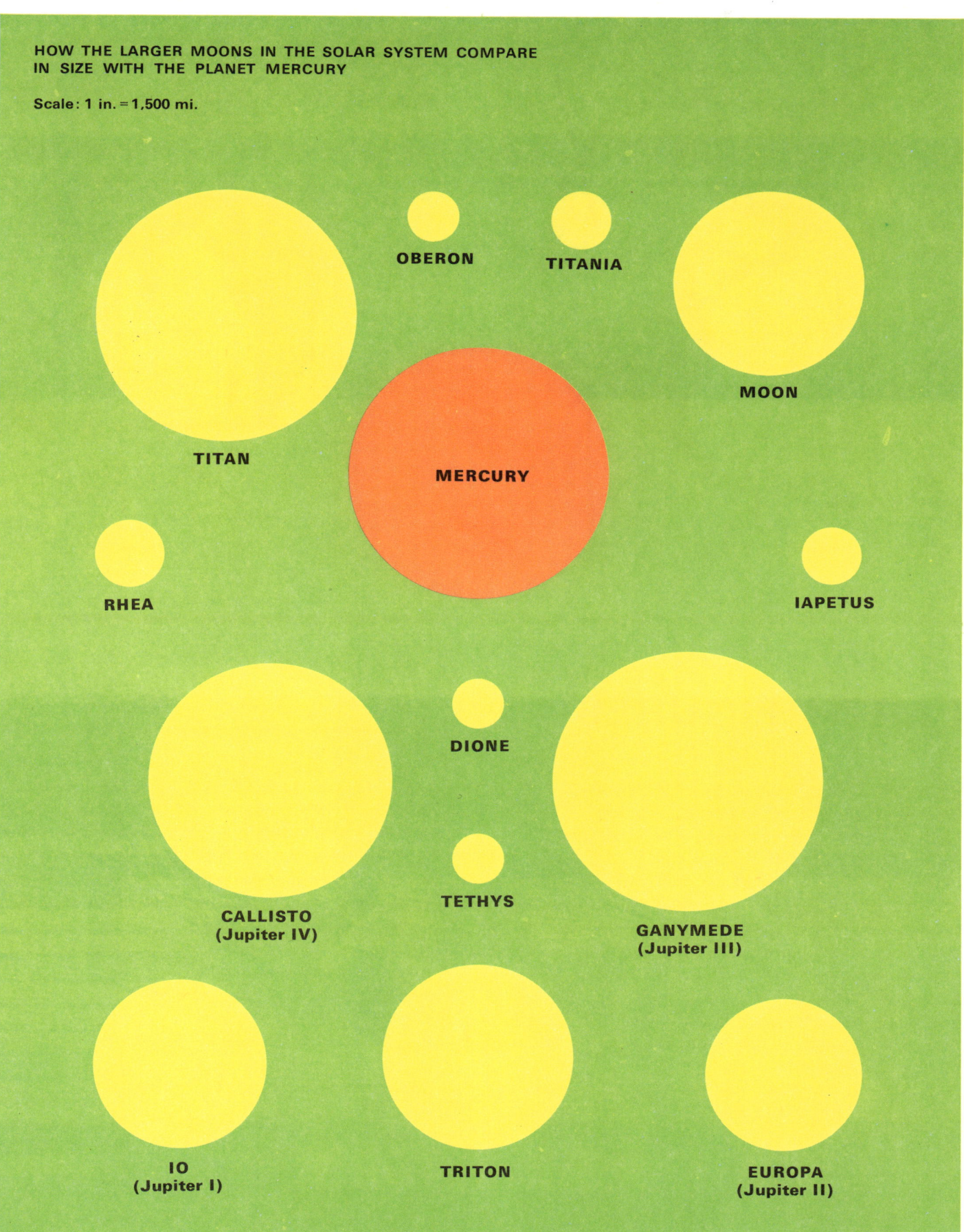

HOW THE LARGER MOONS IN THE SOLAR SYSTEM COMPARE IN SIZE WITH THE PLANET MERCURY

Scale: 1 in. = 1,500 mi.

OBERON

TITANIA

MOON

TITAN

MERCURY

RHEA

IAPETUS

DIONE

CALLISTO
(Jupiter IV)

TETHYS

GANYMEDE
(Jupiter III)

IO
(Jupiter I)

TRITON

EUROPA
(Jupiter II)

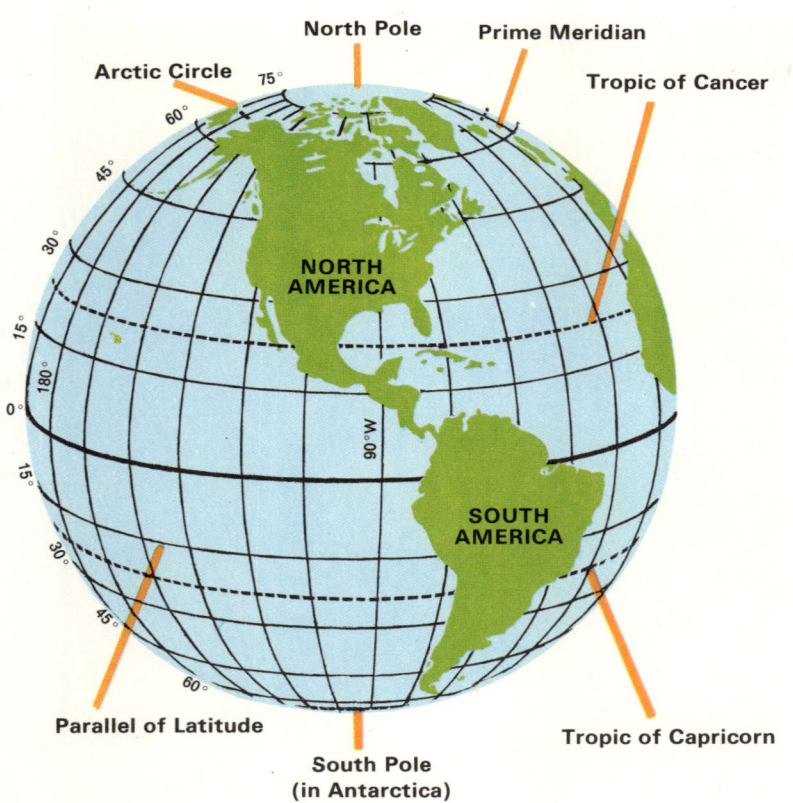

Arctic Circle · North Pole · Prime Meridian · Tropic of Cancer · NORTH AMERICA · SOUTH AMERICA · Parallel of Latitude · South Pole (in Antarctica) · Tropic of Capricorn

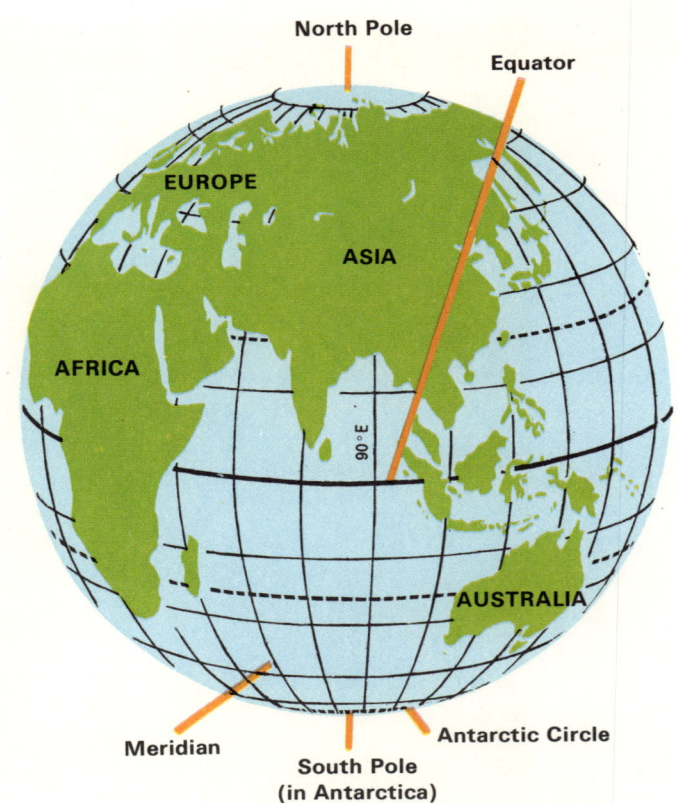

North Pole · Equator · EUROPE · ASIA · AFRICA · AUSTRALIA · Meridian · South Pole (in Antarctica) · Antarctic Circle

EARTH FIGURES

Diameter of earth at equator: 7,926.68 miles.

Circumference of earth at equator: 24,901.8 miles.

Diameter of earth from pole to pole: 7,900 miles.

Circumference of earth through poles: 24,860.49 miles.

Length of a degree of latitude at the equator: 68·704 miles.

(The length of a degree of latitude would be the same everywhere if the earth were a perfect sphere. The slight flattening at the poles makes the length of a degree of latitude slightly greater in the polar regions.)

Length of a degree of longitude at the equator: 69.17 English miles (60 geographical miles). The length of a degree of longitude is greatest at the equator. It decreases gradually towards the poles.

Area of earth's surface: 196,950,284 square miles.

Volume of earth: about 259,902,237,000 cubic miles.

Mass of earth: 5,882,000,000,000,000,000,000 tons.

Time needed for one rotation on its axis: 23 hours, 56 minutes, 4.09 seconds. (This period of time is called the sidereal, or star, day. The day we use in our calendar is the solar, or sun, day which averages 24 hours.)

Time needed for one journey around the sun: 365 days, 6 hours, 9 minutes, 9.5 seconds.

Speed of a point on the equator as the earth rotates: about $17\frac{1}{2}$ miles per minute.

Average speed at which the earth travels around the sun: $18\frac{1}{2}$ miles per second.

Speed at which the sun is carrying the earth around the centre of the Milky Way galaxy: 170 miles per second.

Speed at which the galaxy is drifting through space: more than 170 miles per second.

FACTS ABOUT OUR GLOBE

No one can ever see the sun straight overhead if he is north of the Tropic of Cancer or south of the Tropic of Capricorn.

'Due east towards the rising sun' is a well-known phrase, but actually the sun, except at the equator, rises due east only at the spring and autumn equinoxes—about March 21st and September 23rd. It sets due west when it rises due east.

At the North Pole, where there are 186 days of constant daylight and 179 days of night, the sun is never more than $23\frac{1}{2}°$ above the horizon; at the South Pole, on the other hand, the sun does not set for 179 continuous days and instead there are 186 days of night.

At the equinoxes, the noon shadow of a person in Latitude 45° N. or Latitude 45° S. is exactly as long as the person is tall.

If your home is exactly halfway between the North Pole and the equator, in Europe you may live in France, Italy, Yugoslavia, Rumania, or the U.S.S.R. In Asia your home may be in the U.S.S.R., Mongolia, Manchuria or at the very northern tip of Japan. In North America your home may be in Oregon, Idaho, Montana, South Dakota, Minnesota or Maine, in the United States.

If you live halfway between the equator and the South Pole, your home would have to be in Argentina, Chile or New Zealand.

The southernmost town in the world is Punta Arenas, in southern Chile, South America.

The northernmost town in the world is Etah, Greenland.

If you could dig a hole from Shanghai, China, straight through the centre of the earth, you would come out not far from Buenos Aires in Argentina.

If you could dig a hole straight through the centre of the earth from New York, you would come out in the Indian Ocean west of Australia.

Rome and Madrid are almost due east of Chicago, Illinois.

If you travelled due east from New Orleans, Louisiana, in the U.S., you would reach Cairo in Egypt and come close to Shanghai in China.

The great cities of London, Berlin, Moscow, Leningrad, Copenhagen, Amsterdam, Rotterdam, Hamburg, Glasgow, Oslo and Stockholm are all farther north than any part of the United States except Alaska.

If you travelled straight south from Vancouver Island, Canada, you would reach no land till you came to Antarctica.

If you travelled straight north from Belem (Pará), Brazil, near the mouth of the Amazon River, you would reach no land till you came to Greenland.

It is possible to sail all the way around the world along the parallel 60° S. Your journey would be half as long as a trip around the world on the equator. It would be roughly as long as a trip from the South Pole to the North Pole along the meridian. It would also be as long as a trip around the world at Latitude 60° N.

The meridian 170° W. reaches from the North Pole almost to the South Pole without hitting any land except some of the small Pacific islands.

The International Date Line, which follows the 180th meridian most of the way, avoids all large land areas.

All of the following 19 countries of Europe together do not take up quite as much space on the earth as Alaska: Albania, Andorra, Austria, Belgium, Britain, Bulgaria, Denmark, Greece, Hungary, Ireland, Liechtenstein, Luxembourg, Monaco, the Netherlands, Portugal, Rumania, San Marino, Switzerland and the Vatican City.

The world's super-giant country, the U.S.S.R., is larger than the whole continent of South America.

Asia could hold both North and South America with room to spare.

In the world's largest city, Tokyo, there are almost as many people as there are in the whole continent of Australia.

Europe is by far the most densely populated continent. With the exception of the principality of Monaco, the Netherlands has more people per square mile than any other country in the world. The two most densely populated areas in the world are Hong Kong, and Macao which is off the southern coast of China.

EXTENT OF LAND AND WATER ON THE EARTH'S SURFACE

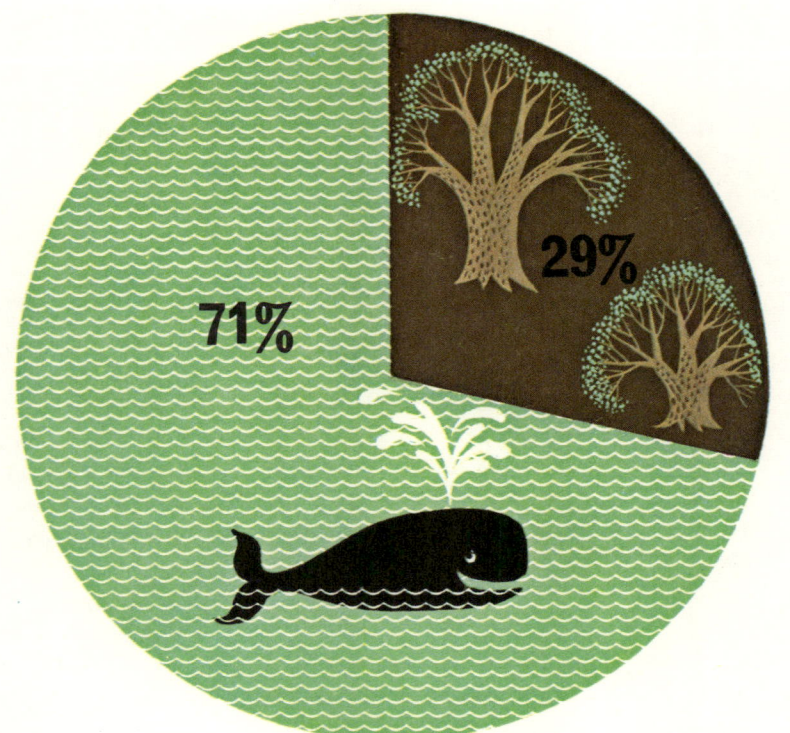

THE EARTH AS A WHOLE

NORTHERN HEMISPHERE

SOUTHERN HEMISPHERE

THE SEVEN CONTINENTS

CONTINENT	AREA IN SQUARE MILES (round figures)	POPULATION (round figures)
Asia	17,000,000	1,665,000,000
Africa	11,683,000	310,000,000
North America	9,300,000	265,000,000
South America	6,800,000	140,000,000
Antarctica	5,300,000	seasonal, up to 1,500
Europe	3,850,000	560,000,000
(Oceania, including Australia)	3,451,000	17,500,000

Comparative sizes

0 1000 2000 3000 4000 5000

SCALE—miles

Asia   Africa   North America   South America   Antarctica   Europe   Australia

THE WORLD'S LARGEST ISLANDS

Island	Ocean	Area in Sq. Mi. (approx.)	Population (approx.)
Greenland	Arctic	840,000	40,000
New Guinea	Pacific	340,000	2,560,000
Borneo (Kalimantan)	Pacific	290,000	4,000,000
Madagascar	Indian	241,000	6,500,000
Baffin Island	Arctic	237,000	3,000
Sumatra	Indian	165,000	14,600,000
Honshū Japan	Pacific	88,000	71,354,000
Great Britain	Atlantic	84,186	54,895,000
Victoria	Arctic	80,000	42,000
Ellesmere	Arctic	77,000	60
Celebes (Sulawesi)	Indian	73,000	7,000,000
South Island, N.Z.	Pacific	58,092	783,327
Java	Pacific	48,882	60,909,000
North Island, N.Z.	Pacific	44,281	1,893,592
Cuba	Atlantic	44,000	6,743,000
Newfoundland	Atlantic	42,750	505,000
Luzon, Philippine Islands	Pacific	41,000	7,500,000
Iceland	Atlantic	40,000	176,000
Mindanao, Philippine Islands	Pacific	36,900	1,900,000
Ireland	Atlantic	31,839	4,368,772
Hokkaido, Japan	Pacific	30,000	5,039,000
Novaya Zemlya	Arctic	30,000	0
Hispaniola (Haiti & Dominican Rep.)	Atlantic/Caribbean	29,500	6,519,000
Tasmania	Pacific	26,215	371,217
Banks Island	Arctic	26,000	0
Ceylon	Indian	25,332	9,612,000

THE EIGHT LARGEST ISLANDS

Comparative sizes

0 200 400 600 800 1000
SCALE—miles

Greenland   New Guinea   Borneo   Madagascar   Baffin Island   Sumatra   Honshu   Great Britain

THE SEVEN SEAS

Much has been written about the seven seas. There are only four oceans. To bring the count up to seven, the Atlantic must be divided into the North Atlantic and the South Atlantic, the Pacific must be divided into the North Pacific and the South Pacific, and the water surrounding Antarctica is called the Southern Ocean. The remaining two oceans are the Indian and Arctic Oceans.

In ancient times people spoke of seven seas, too, but their seven seas were bodies of water in the Old World. They were the Mediterranean Sea, the Red Sea, the Persian Gulf, the China Sea, the Indian Ocean, the East African Ocean and the West African Ocean.

OCEAN	Area (in sq. mi.)	Average Depth (in ft.)	Greatest Depth (in ft.)
PACIFIC	63,800,000	14,000	36,198
ATLANTIC	31,830,000	12,880	27,498
INDIAN	28,350,000	13,000	26,400
ARCTIC	5,440,000	4,200	17,850
SOUTHERN OCEAN	5,731,350	4,920	18,850

SEA TREASURE

The oceans are a great storehouse of food. Fishermen take over 50 million tons of fish each year from the oceans. Vast amounts of shellfish are caught, too. And the algae growing in the 'pastures of the sea' are a possible future source of food.

Whales, seals and walruses furnish food, but whales are also valuable for their oil and whalebone, seals for their fur and walruses for the ivory of their tusks. Sponges are gathered from the floors of warm seas. Pearls and precious coral come from warm seas, too.

The seas are very rich in chemicals. In every cubic mile of ocean water there are about 175 million tons, worth more than 2 million pounds. Most abundant, of course, is salt. Among the many other chemicals are compounds of magnesium, sulphur, calcium, potassium, iron, copper, lead molybdenum, silver, vanadium, nickel, mercury and gold.

There are more than 4 million tons of magnesium in a cubic mile of ocean water. Large quantities are being removed and used in industry.

The ocean contains 99 per cent of the world's supply of bromine. There is about one pound of bromine in 2,000 gallons of ocean water. It is being removed and used for high-grade petrol.

More minerals are constantly being deposited in the mineral 'bank' of the oceans; rivers carry about 160 million tons to the sea each year.

On the ocean floor there is treasure from shipwrecked vessels. But this forms only a tiny part of the wealth of the seven seas.

FAMOUS OCEAN CROSSINGS

In 1819 the *Savannah,* the first ship to partially use steam in crossing an ocean, made the trip from Savannah, Georgia, U.S.A., to Liverpool, in 26 days. The world's first nuclear-powered merchant ship was named after this old ship.

In 1827 the Dutch paddle boat, *Curacao,* was the first power vessel to cross the Atlantic. The journey, from Rotterdam to the West Indies, took 22 days.

In 1838 the packet ship *Sirius* made the first transatlantic crossing under continuous steam power. The journey from Ireland to the United States took 18 days.

In 1854 the clipper *James Baines* set a record by crossing the Atlantic from Boston to Liverpool in 12 days, 6 hrs.

In 1919 John Alcock and Arthur Whitten-Brown flew from Newfoundland to Ireland non-stop in 16 hrs, 12 min.

In 1927 Charles Lindbergh made the first solo Atlantic flight in his single-engine aircraft *Spirit of St Louis* non-stop from New York to Paris in 33 hrs, 30 min.

In 1927 two Americans, Hegenberger and Maitland, flew from Oakland, near San Francisco, to Honolulu in 25 hrs, 50 min. Their aircraft was a 3-engined Fokker monoplane.

In 1928 Hermann Köhl (Germany), Baron von Hühnefeld (Germany) and Flight Captain James Fitzmaurice (Ireland) were first to fly the Atlantic from east to west.

In 1929 two Spaniards, Ignacio Jimenez and Francisco Iglesias made a non-stop flight from Seville in Spain to Bahia on the west coast of Brazil.

In 1936 the dirigible (airship) *Hindenburg* flew over the Atlantic in 42 hrs, 53 min.

In 1952 the ocean liner *United States* crossed the Atlantic in 3 days, 10 hrs, 40 min.

In 1958 the U.S. atomic-powered submarine *Nautilus* crossed the Arctic Ocean by travelling under the polar ice-cap. In the same year the U.S. submarine *Skate* became the first vessel to travel across the Atlantic and back under water without surfacing.

In 1959 a Boeing 707 flew from New York to Shannon in Ireland in 5 hrs, 5 min.

In 1960 the U.S. submarine *Triton* travelled all the way around the world without surfacing. The trip took 84 days.

OCEAN DEEPS

In the floors of the oceans there are deep furrows called trenches, troughs or deeps. The deepest are in the region shown in the upper map. Deepest of all is the Marianas Trench, which goes down to 36,198 feet. It is deeper than Mount Everest, the world's highest mountain, is tall. The deepest trench in the Atlantic Ocean is the Puerto Rico Trench which, in one place called the Milwaukee Depth, goes down to 30,246 feet.

Nobody knows why these trenches are there. At one time it was thought that they were the river valleys of old continents now covered by the sea. But some present-day scientists think that they really represent cracks in the earth's crust due to volcanic explosions, though there is some disagreement about this.

The scientists who suggest that the trenches are cracks in the earth's crust, base their theories on two interesting facts: most of these trenches, or deeps, are found in the 'earthquake belt' round the world, and they nearly always run parallel to a curving line of islands, submerged ridges or continental coastline.

The deepest ocean trenches are:

Pacific Ocean—Marianas Trench, 36,198 feet. (This is the greatest known ocean depth, located just off the Philippines).

Atlantic Ocean—Puerto Rico Trench, 27,498 feet.

Indian Ocean—Diamantina Trench, 26,400 feet.

Arctic Ocean—greatest depth is 17,850 feet.

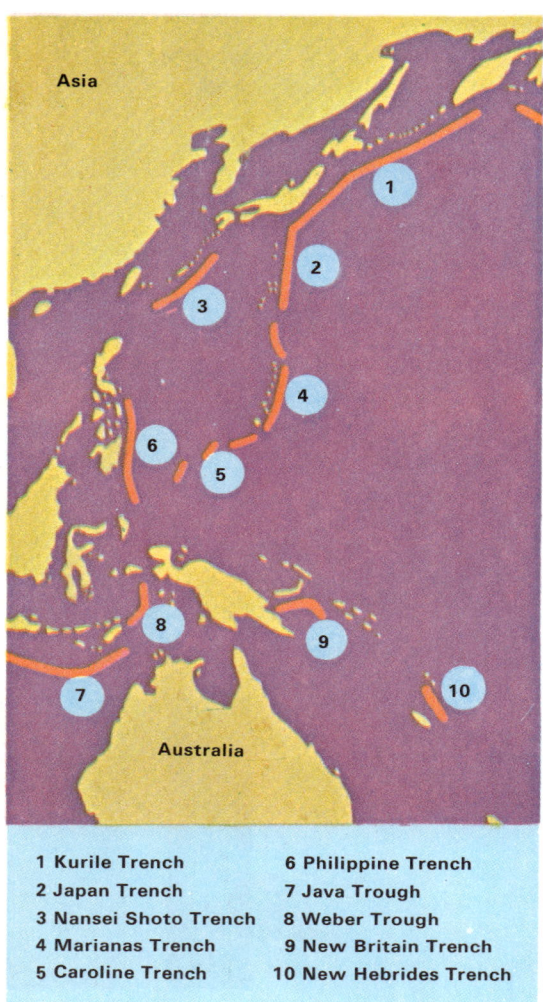

1 Kurile Trench	6 Philippine Trench
2 Japan Trench	7 Java Trough
3 Nansei Shoto Trench	8 Weber Trough
4 Marianas Trench	9 New Britain Trench
5 Caroline Trench	10 New Hebrides Trench

MOUNTAINS OF THE SEA

Many mountains rise from the floor of the sea. Some are volcanoes; others are folded mountains.

Down the middle of the Atlantic Ocean there is a great mountain chain longer than any mountain chain on land. It is called the Atlantic Ridge. This 10,000 mile long mountain chain is also broad—broader than the Andes. Some of its peaks rise above the sea to form islands. The Azores are peaks of the chain. Other islands which are peaks of the Atlantic Ridge are shown on the map.

There are similar mountain ranges in the Pacific and Indian oceans, but they are not so long. Extending across the Pacific Ocean from Hawaii to the Marianas there is a range of flat-topped mountains all far below the surface. How they came to be flat-topped is a mystery.

Many of the mountains of the sea are far older than any mountains on land. Under the sea, mountains are worn down very, very slowly. They are protected there from the wind and quick changes in temperature which help tear down mountains on land.

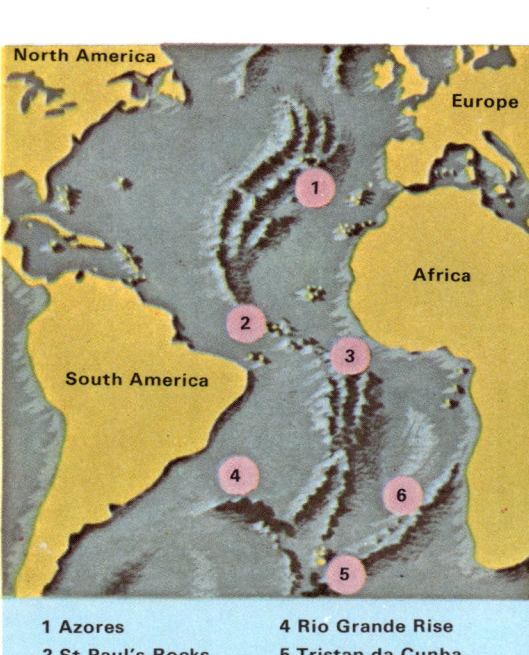

1 Azores	4 Rio Grande Rise
2 St Paul's Rocks	5 Tristan da Cunha
3 Ascension Isle	6 Walvis Ridge

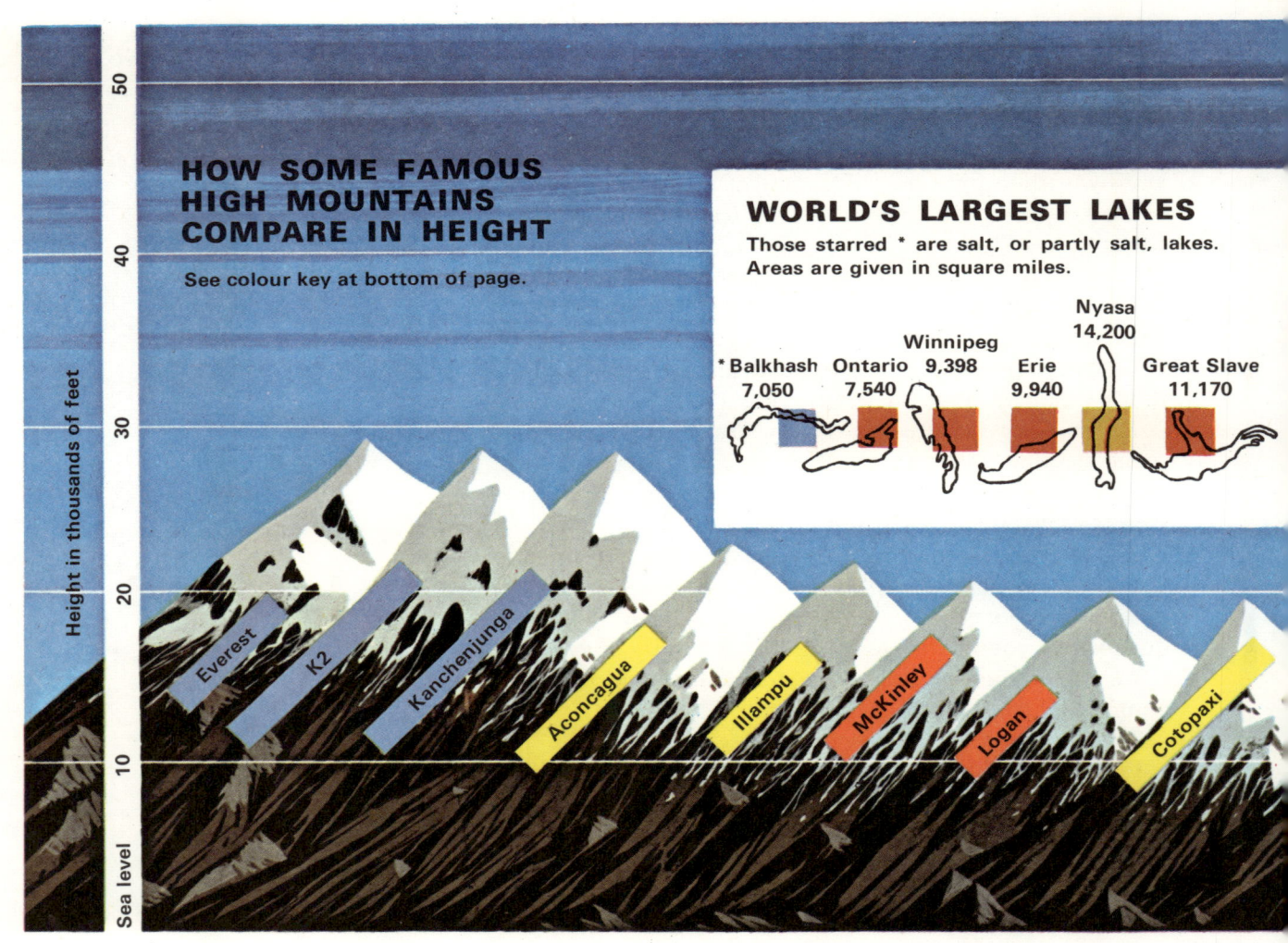

HOW SOME FAMOUS HIGH MOUNTAINS COMPARE IN HEIGHT

See colour key at bottom of page.

Height in thousands of feet

50

40

30

20

10

Sea level

Everest
K2
Kanchenjunga
Aconcagua
Illampu
McKinley
Logan
Cotopaxi

WORLD'S LARGEST LAKES

Those starred * are salt, or partly salt, lakes.
Areas are given in square miles.

Nyasa
14,200

Winnipeg
9,398

* Balkhash   Ontario   Erie   Great Slave
  7,050   7,540   9,398   9,940   11,170

COLOUR KEY

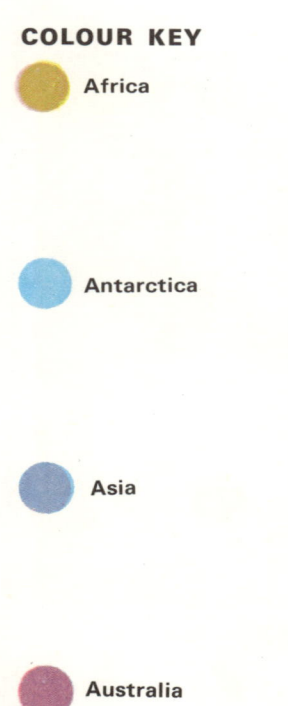

Africa

Antarctica

Asia

Australia

WORLD'S HIGHEST WATERFALLS

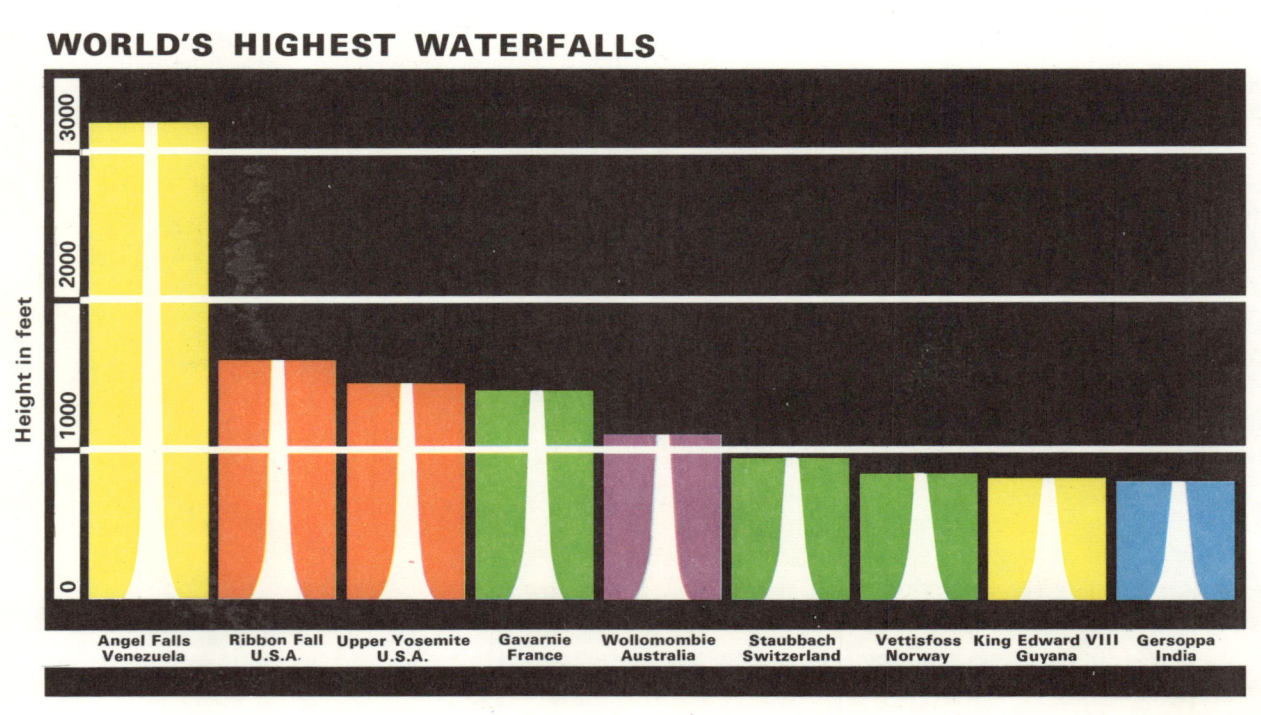

Height in feet

3000

2000

1000

0

Angel Falls
Venezuela

Ribbon Fall
U.S.A.

Upper Yosemite
U.S.A.

Gavarnie
France

Wollomombie
Australia

Staubbach
Switzerland

Vettisfoss
Norway

King Edward VIII
Guyana

Gersoppa
India

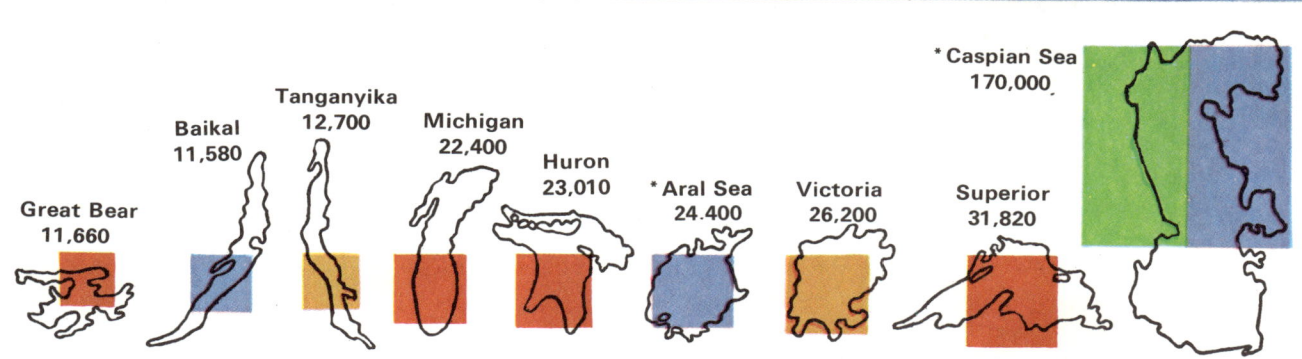

* Caspian Sea
170,000

Baikal
11,580

Tanganyika
12,700

Michigan
22,400

Huron
23,010

Great Bear
11,660

* Aral Sea
24,400

Victoria
26,200

Superior
31,820

Kilimanjaro
Elbrus
Orizaba
Kenya
Ruwenzori
Mont Blanc
Markham
Matterhorn
Erebus
Kosciusko

WORLD'S LONGEST RIVERS

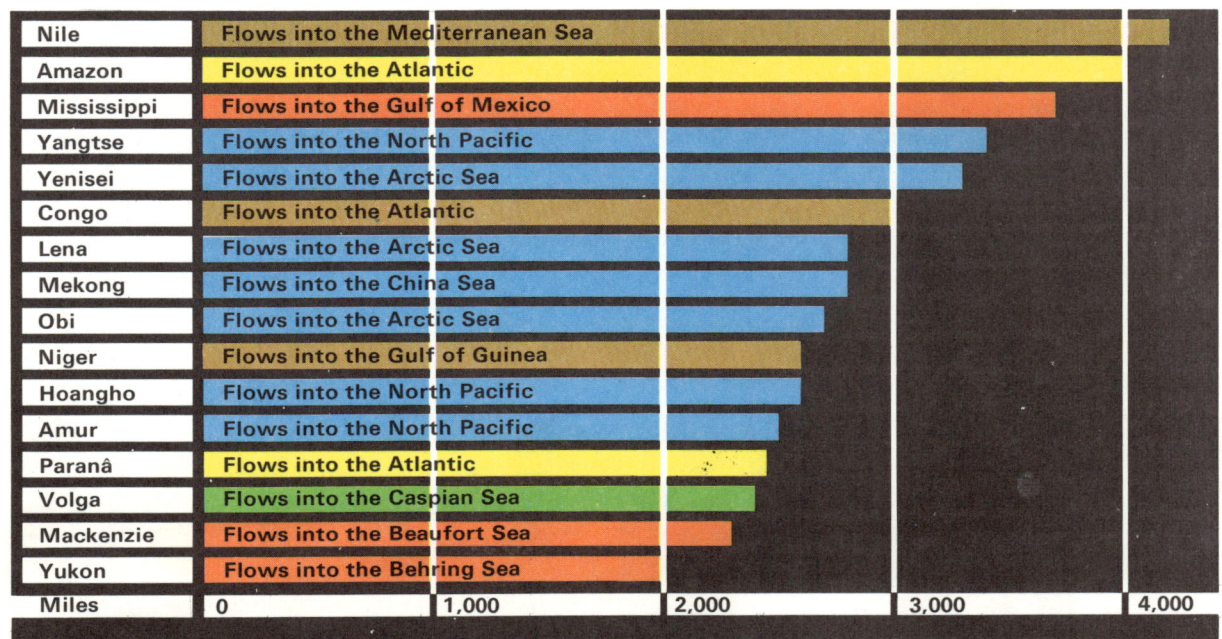

Nile	Flows into the Mediterranean Sea	
Amazon	Flows into the Atlantic	
Mississippi	Flows into the Gulf of Mexico	
Yangtse	Flows into the North Pacific	
Yenisei	Flows into the Arctic Sea	
Congo	Flows into the Atlantic	
Lena	Flows into the Arctic Sea	
Mekong	Flows into the China Sea	
Obi	Flows into the Arctic Sea	
Niger	Flows into the Gulf of Guinea	
Hoangho	Flows into the North Pacific	
Amur	Flows into the North Pacific	
Paranâ	Flows into the Atlantic	
Volga	Flows into the Caspian Sea	
Mackenzie	Flows into the Beaufort Sea	
Yukon	Flows into the Behring Sea	
Miles	0 1,000 2,000 3,000 4,000	

COLOUR KEY

 Europe

 New Zealand

 North America

 South America

Shale

Sandstone

Limestone

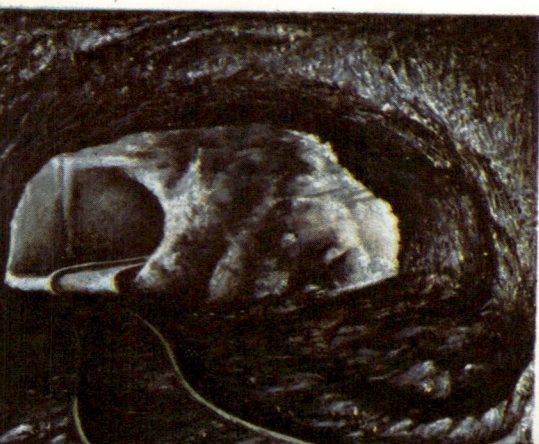

Coal

ROCKS

Wherever we are in the world, below us is solid rock—sometimes miles below the surface of a great ocean, sometimes buried by many feet of soil. Soil is the result of weathering of rocks. It accumulates by a long slow process which is going on all the time. It is from the destruction of rocks that new ones are formed. As the rocks are broken down, the debris is carried by wind and water into the valleys and transported to the sea. Here the sediment piles up, getting thicker and thicker. Water trickling through the layers may carry minerals which gradually cement all the particles together. A change in sea level eventually results in sedimentary rocks, for this is what rocks so formed are called, being exposed at the surface. Some examples of sedimentary rocks are:—conglomerate, made up of gravel and pebbles cemented together; sandstone, making up 20% of all this type of rock; and shales which make up 50% of sedimentary rocks.

A well known conglomerate is called 'Hertfordshire Puddingstone' which is found in the London area.

Sandstone is usually made up of small quartz particles. Typical colours of sandstones are white, pink, brown and red. Shales consist of very fine grains of clay. They originate in lake beds, deltas and bays.

Limestone is also a sedimentary rock and is often made up entirely of animal remains. The chalk which makes up the White Cliffs of Dover is a limestone which consists mostly of dying organisms called foraminifera.

The coal we burn on our fires is also a sedimentary rock. The coal found in Great Britain was formed some 270–300 million years ago. In these times there were luxuriant swamps with enormous 'scale-trees' growing to over 100 feet, while relatives of our horse tails grew up to 40 feet. Many types of fern also grew in these swamps. Gradually the areas of swamp were invaded by the sea which deposited sand and mud on the layers of dead vegetation. This vegetation was gradually compacted by the weight of the sediment into the coal we know today. The sea would then retreat and the whole process would be repeated time and time again. As previously mentioned, sedimentary rocks are mostly formed from the break-down of other rocks—but how then were the first rocks formed? They were formed from the weathering of other types of rocks known as igneous rocks, from the Latin word *'ignis'* meaning 'fire'. The oldest known rock

in the world is an igneous rock called granite from Southern Africa, dated as 3,400 million years old. There are undoubtedly older rocks still to be found.

The igneous rocks are formed as the result of what is called igneous activity. Examples of such activity are volcanoes, lava flows and hot springs. Underground heat is the cause of these phenomena and others associated with the birth of igneous rocks. Deep down in the earth the rock is in molten form called magma. Occasionally this forces its way through cracks in the earth's surface and pours out as a lava flow or continues to build up material around the central vent to form a volcano.

Basalt is a typical basic lava which can spread a great distance from the original vent. The famous hexagonal columns of the Giant's Causeway in Antrim, Northern Ireland, and of Fingal's Cave on the Isle of Staffa, Scotland, are made of basalt. Basalt is very fine textured rock, characteristic of an igneous rock which has been formed when magma cools quickly at the surface of the earth. When magma does not reach the surface but cools below ground, the rocks formed have a coarse texture. An example of this type of rock is granite, in which it is possible to see, with the naked eye, the various minerals which go to make up the rock.

There is one other great group of rocks, called metamorphic rocks, which are formed when other sedimentary or igneous rocks are changed by heat and pressure. The word metamorphic comes from the Greek, meaning 'changed completely'. When the great masses of molten magma cool below the surface, their heat and the pressure exerted by them on the surrounding rocks causes these original rocks to change. Some examples of metamorphic rocks are slates, gneiss and marble. Slates are formed from shales. Some of the most famous slate quarries are in North Wales. Gneiss originates from granite and possibly some sedimentary rocks while marble comes from limestone. If the original limestone is pure, then a white marble such as the well-known Carrara Marble from Italy will result. If, as is more usual, impurities are present, the marble may well be any colour.

The geologist can reconstruct the history of the earth from the earliest time, by studying the various rocks. He knows what conditions existed when certain types of rocks were formed, whether there were volcanoes in the area, or if the rocks have been changed by immense heat and pressure from their original type.

Basalt

Granite

Gneiss

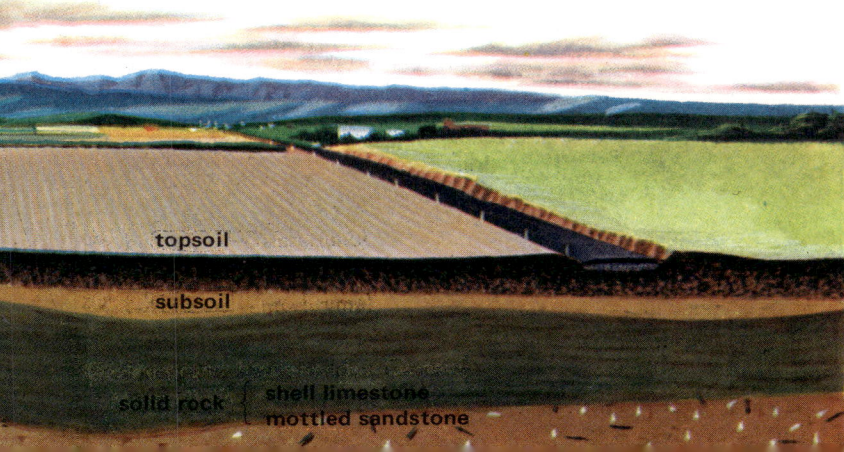

topsoil

subsoil

solid rock { shell limestone
mottled sandstone

Marble

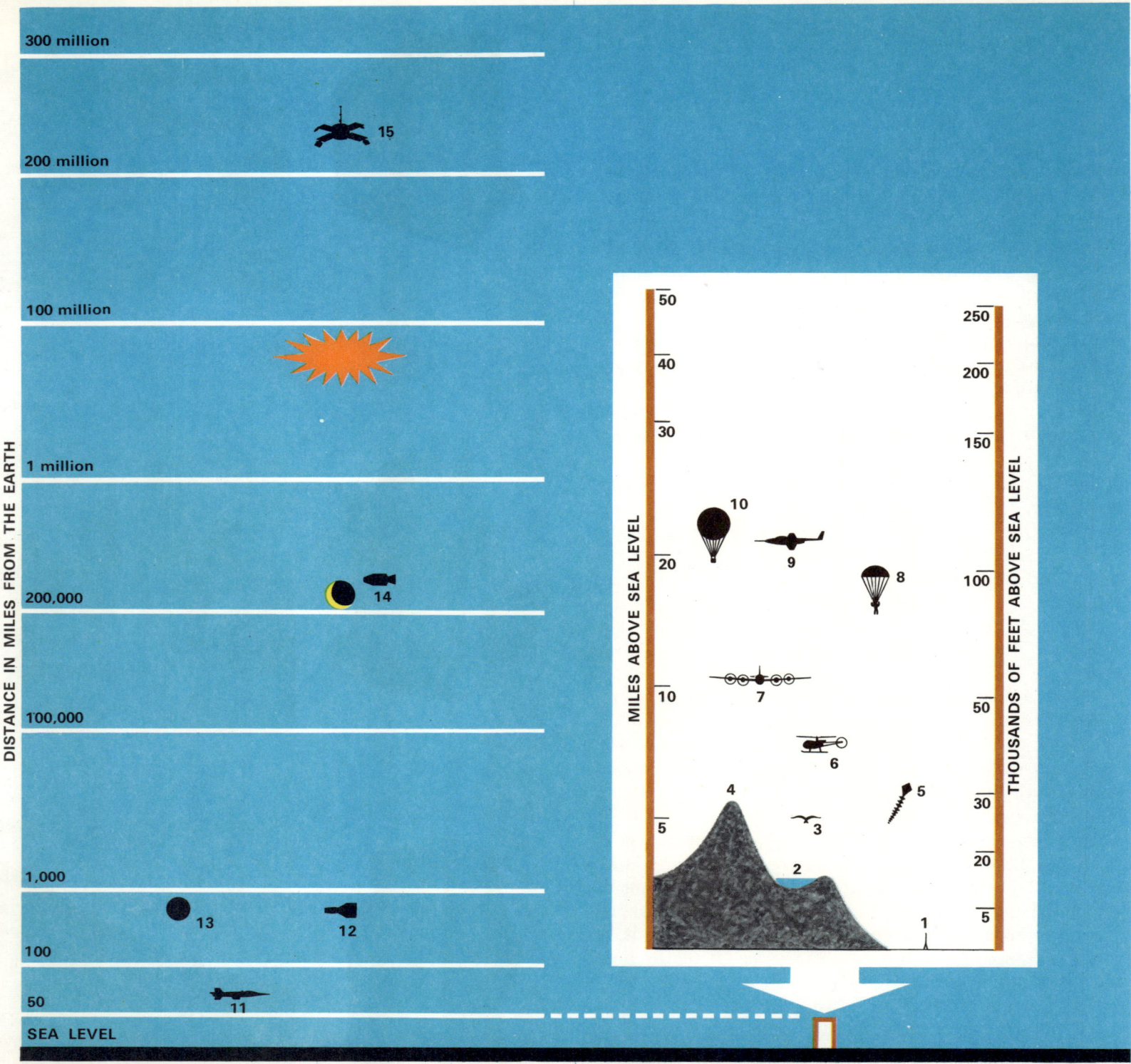

RECORD HIGHS AND DISTANCES

1. Highest structure built by man—television tower between Fargo and Blanchard, North Dakota, U.S.A. — 2,063 feet
2. Highest lake—Lake Titicaca — 12,506 feet
3. Highest altitude at which birds have been seen to fly — 26,902 feet
4. Highest mountain peak—Mt Everest — 29,028 feet
5. Highest kite (kites in tandem) ascent — 31,955 feet
6. Highest helicopter ascent — 36,027 feet
7. Highest propeller aircraft ascent — 56,046 feet
8. Highest parachute jump — 102,200 feet
9. Highest jet plane ascent — 113,890 feet
10. Highest manned balloon ascent — 123,800 feet
11. Highest rocket aircraft ascent (X–15) — 67.08 miles
12. Highest point reached by manned spacecraft in orbit (Gemini II) — 851 miles
13. Highest unmanned balloon (Satellite Echo 2 was inflated in space) — 922 miles
14. Highest point reached by manned spacecraft in non-orbital flight (Apollo 8) — 240,000 miles
15. Farthest distance reached by artificial satellite (Mariner 4) — 234 million miles

44

RECORD LOWS

1. Depth reached by skin diver with aqualung — 397 feet
2. Depth to which diver in full flexible diving suit can go — 728 feet
3. Deepest level for submarines (non-research vessels) over 800 feet (the record is classified information)
4. Lowest point on continents— Dead Sea — 1,286 feet below sea level
5. Deepest descent of bathysphere — 3,028 feet
6. Depth to which sunlight can penetrate — 3,300 feet
7. Depth to which whales can dive — 3,700 feet
8. Deepest descent of benthyscope — 4,500 feet
9. Deepest well for water (near Blackall, Queensland, Australia) — 7,009 feet
10. Deepest mine (Boksburg, Transvaal) — 11,246 feet
11. Deepest oil well (Texas, U.S.A.) — 25,340 feet
12. Deepest descent of bathoscaphe — 35,802 feet
13. Deepest level at which animal life has been found — 35,802 feet
14. Deepest ocean depth (Marianas Trench, Pacific Ocean) — 36,198 feet

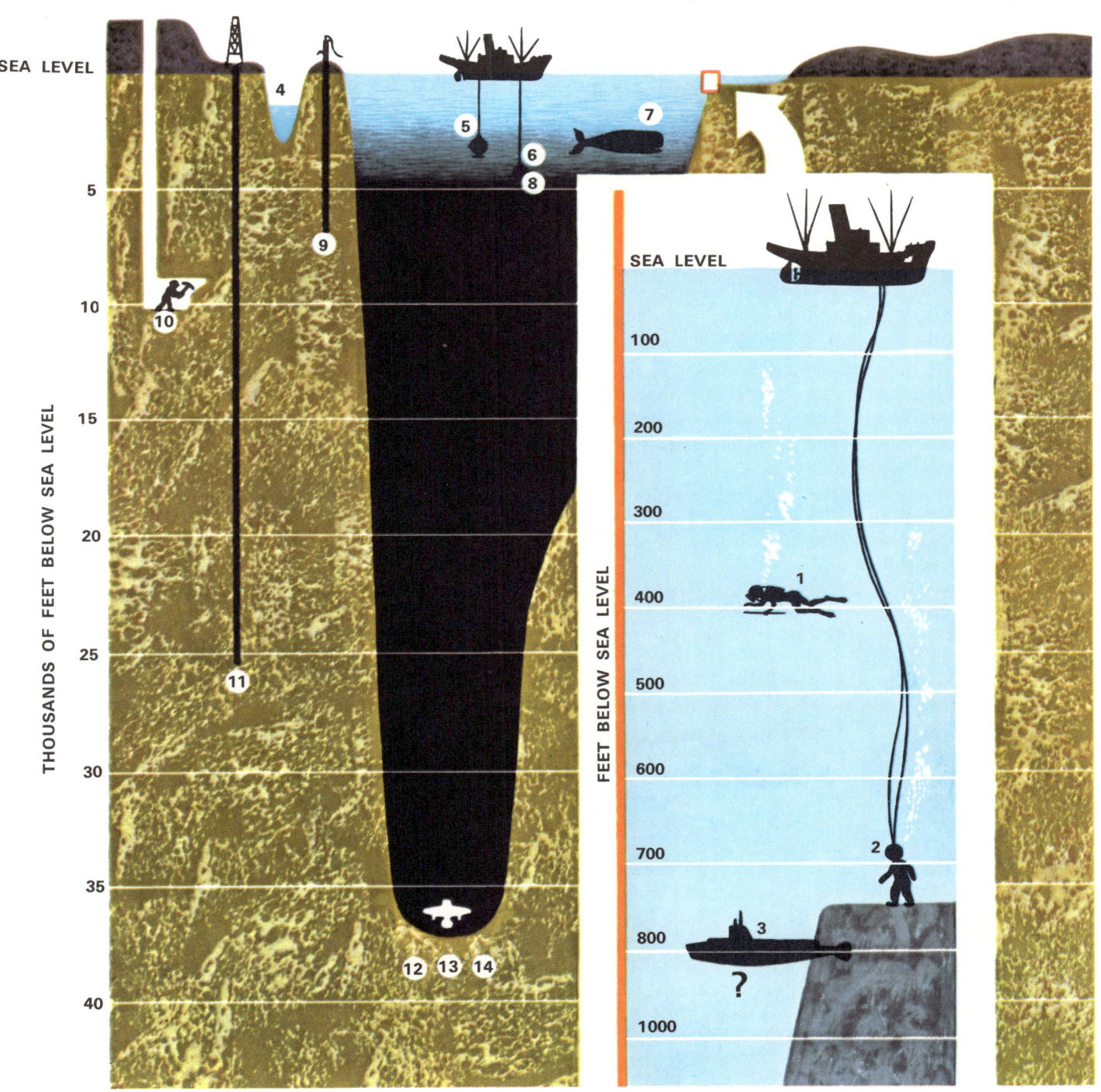

WEATHER TERMS

AIR PRESSURE. The force with which the air pushes down. Winds are caused by differences in air pressure.

ANTICYCLONE. The movement of air outward from the centre of an area of high pressure.

BLIZZARD. A snowstorm with a strong wind.

CEILING. The height of the base of any clouds which are lower than 9,750 feet and which cover more than half the sky. If there is a heavy fog resting on the ground, the ceiling is zero. If there are no clouds in sight, or if the clouds are above 9,750 feet, the ceiling is 'unlimited.'

CLIMATE. Average weather conditions over a long period of time.

CLOUDBURST. A storm in which very heavy rain falls in a short time.

CLOUD SEEDING. The dropping of crystals of sodium iodide or some similar chemical on clouds to make them drop some of their moisture.

COLD FRONT. The boundary between a mass of cool or cold air and one of warmer air at which the cooler air is pushing its way under the warmer air.

COLD WAVE. Cold weather that lasts for several days.

CONDENSATION. The changing of a substance from vapour to a liquid state.

CYCLONE. The movement of air in towards the centre of an area of low pressure—often called a depression.

DEW. Drops of water that form on objects from the condensation of water vapour in the air. Dew does not fall; it is formed where you find it.

DUST STORM. A storm in which strong winds carry great amounts of dry topsoil.

FOG. A cloud close to the ground made up of very tiny droplets of water around small soot or dust particles.

FROST. Crystals of ice that form on objects from the condensation of water vapour in the air. Frost, like dew, is formed where you find it.

GLAZE. A coating of ice formed when rain freezes on the surfaces it strikes; e.g., on the branches of trees and bushes.

HAIL. Balls made up of layers of ice and snow, formed when raindrops freeze high above the earth and move up and down in the clouds before they fall to the ground.

HIGH. The movement of air outward from a region of high air pressure; an anticyclone.

HUMIDITY. The amount of water vapour in the air.

HURRICANE. A great windstorm covering hundreds of square miles and often lasting a whole day. Hurricanes originate in warm regions over the oceans. They are often called 'tropical cyclones.'

ICE STORM. A storm in which glaze forms on the branches of trees, telephone wires, bushes and other such objects. Often the weight of the ice does much damage.

ISOBAR. A line on a weather map joining places having equal air pressure at a particular time.

ISOTHERM. A line on a weather map connecting places with the same temperature.

JET STREAM. A swiftly moving current of air some 400 miles wide and 4 miles deep, and from 20,000 to 40,000 feet above the ground. The speed of the air in a jet stream may reach 250 miles an hour. Aeroplanes often take advantage of a jet stream to increase their speed.

LOW. The movement of air inwards towards the centre of

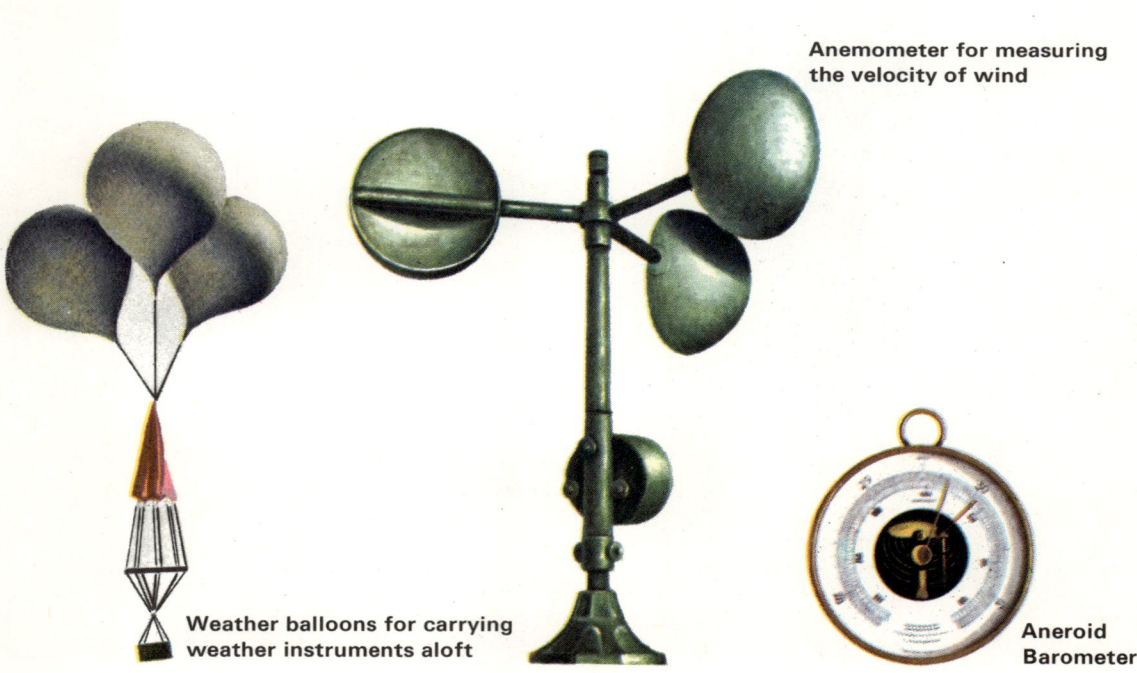

Anemometer for measuring the velocity of wind

Weather balloons for carrying weather instruments aloft

Aneroid Barometer

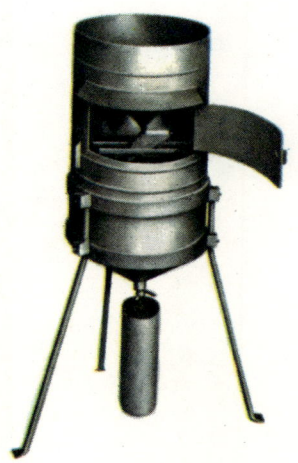

Tipping bucket rain gauge (this measures rainfall)

an area of low air pressure; a cyclone.

MILLIBAR. A unit of pressure. On weather maps the air pressure may be marked in both inches (the height of the mercury in a mercury barometer) and millibars.

OCCLUSION. When, in a depression, the cold front undercuts the warm sector, gradually lifting it from contact with the earth's surface.

PRECIPITATION. Moisture that falls from clouds: rain, snow and sleet or hail.

RELATIVE HUMIDITY. The amount of water vapour in the air in comparison with the total amount that the air could hold if fully saturated.

SLEET. Small balls of ice formed when rain freezes as it falls.

SMOG. A combination of smoke and fog.

TEMPERATURE-HUMIDITY INDEX. A figure taking into account both the temperature and the humidity at a given time. Very few people are uncomfortable because of the heat and humidity if the index figure is 70 or below. Many are uncomfortable if it reaches 75. And almost everyone is uncomfortable if the index climbs to 79 or above.

THUNDERSTORM. A storm in which there are strong upward currents of air—with thunder and lightning.

TORNADO. A very violent windstorm covering only a small area and moving very fast.

TYPHOON. The name given to a hurricane that originates over the Pacific Ocean.

UNSETTLED WEATHER. Changeable weather with a strong possibility of rain or snow.

WARM FRONT. A boundary between a mass of warm air

Hygrograph
(this records humidity)

Recording
Thermometer

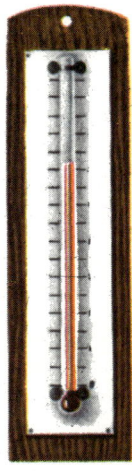

Alcohol
Thermometer

and a mass of cooler air at which the warm air is climbing up over the cooler air.

WEATHER MAP. A map showing weather conditions over a large area and forming a basis for weather predictions.

WIND DIRECTION. The direction *from* which the wind is blowing.

WIND VELOCITY. The speed of wind measured in miles per hour or in knots.

THE BEAUFORT SCALE

Beaufort number	Wind	Effect on Land	Speed in m.p.h.
0	Calm	Smoke rises vertically	Less than 1
1	Light Air	Direction shown by smoke but not by wind vanes	1-3
2	Light breeze	Wind felt on face; leaves rustle; wind vanes move	4-7
3	Gentle breeze	Leaves and twigs in motion; wind extends light flag	8-12
4	Moderate breeze	Raises dust, loose paper and moves small branches	13-18
5	Fresh breeze	Small trees in leaf begin to sway	19-24
6	Strong breeze	Large branches in motion; whistling in telegraph wires; difficulty with umbrellas	25-31
7	Moderate gale	Whole trees in motion; difficult to walk against wind	32-38
8	Fresh gale	Twigs break off trees; progress impeded	39-46
9	Strong gale	Slight structural damage occurs; chimney pots and slates blown off	47-54
10	Whole gale	Trees uprooted and considerable structural damage	55-63
11	Storm	Widespread damage, seldom experienced in England	64-75
12	Hurricane	Winds of this force only encountered in tropical revolving storms	Above 75

NINE CLOUD TYPES

CIRRUS
Delicate wispy white clouds always made of ice crystals. Before sunrise and after sunset, often coloured yellow or red. Average height above ground 25,000 feet.

CIRRO-STRATUS
Thin white clouds forming a gauzy veil that causes haloes around the sun and moon. Never thick enough to prevent shadows. Average height 20,000 feet.

CIRRO-CUMULUS
Small white flakes of clouds forming an even pattern. A sky covered with clouds of this kind often called mackerel-sky. Average height is about 20,000 feet.

CUMULUS
Fluffy towering white clouds with rounded tops and flat bases. Often called fair-weather clouds. Average height of base 1,600 feet. Upper height does not exceed 10,000 feet.

CUMULO-NIMBUS
Towering clouds, often anvil-topped, popularly called 'thunderheads'. May bring heavy showers and hail. Average height of base, 1,600 feet; of top, 20,000 feet.

ALTO-CUMULUS
White or grey clouds forming broken-up layers or patches somewhat like the cirro-cumulus clouds of a mackerel-sky. Average height of base 6,500 feet.

STRATUS
Greyish clouds forming a uniform layer. Similar to fog but not resting on the ground. May produce drizzle. Height of base from near ground to 6,500 feet.

STRATO-CUMULUS
Dull grey clouds forming a layer broken up into large lumpy masses or long rolls. May give wavy look to sky. Height of base from near surface of ground to 6,500 feet.

NIMBO-STRATUS
Dark grey clouds forming a nearly uniform layer over sky. True rain clouds which frequently bring snow in winter. Height of base from near ground to 6,500 feet.

48

STORMS

TORNADOES
Tornadoes occur most often in the spring and early summer months. Tornado winds are the strongest winds known.

HURRICANES
Hurricanes, called typhoons in the lands bordering the Pacific Ocean, occur most often in late summer and early autumn.

THUNDERSTORMS
Thunderstorms are chiefly summer storms. These are the most common storms, and they may be dry but often bring rain or hail.

ICE STORMS
Ice storms occur most often in late autumn and early spring, when it is just cold enough for rain-drops to freeze as they strike solid matter.

BLIZZARDS
Blizzards are winter storms. They are snowstorms with winds strong enough to pile the snow into big drifts.

DUST STORMS
Dust storms are usually summer storms, but may come at any time when the soil is dry enough to be blown about.

NATURAL DISASTERS

A.D.

79   Mt Vesuvius erupted; Pompeii and Herculaneum were destroyed.

1277   Tidal wave flooded the North Sea coast of Europe destroying 50 villages.

1509   Earthquake destroyed part of Constantinople.

1556   Earthquake in Shensi Province, China, killed about 830,000 people.

1570   Tidal wave off the North Sea destroyed all dykes from Holland to Jutland.

1643   Earthquake destroyed Santiago, Chile, killing $\frac{1}{3}$ of the population.

1703   Earthquake destroyed Tokyo and other towns, killing about 150,000 people.

1755   Earthquake destroyed Lisbon killing about 32,000 people.

1783   Earthquake in Calabria, Italy, killed about 29,000 people.

1828   Earthquake in Japan killed about 30,000 people.

1837   Valdivia (Chile) was destroyed by an earthquake.

1855   Earthquake in Tokyo killed about 106,000 people.

1887   Flooding of the River Hwang-ho (China) killed about 900,000 people.

1896   Earthquake on Honshu island (Japan) killed about 27,000 people.

1902   Mont Pele erupted on the island of Martinique, destroyed the town of Saint-Pierre killing about 30,000 people.

1923   Earthquake in Sagami Bay destroyed Tokyo and Yokohama killing about 150,000 people.

1931   The flooding of Yangtse Kiang and Hwang-ho rivers killed hundreds of thousands of people.

1939   Earthquake in Anatolia killed about 32,000 people.

1953   Floods in coastal districts of England and Holland.

1953   Earthquake in Turkey killed about 1,200 people.

1954   Earthquake in Orléansville (Algeria) killed 1,440 people.

1955   Floods in India and Pakistan made about 45,000,000 homeless.

1960   Earthquake in Agadir, Morocco, killed about 12,000 people.

1962   Peruvian avalanche killed more than 3,000 people.

1963   Volcano disaster in Bali; earthquake in Barce, Libya; Skopje destroyed by earthquake; Hurricane Flora struck the Caribbean.

1966   River Arno in Italy overflowed its banks; $\frac{2}{3}$ of Florence was submerged. Estimated £57,000,000 worth of damage done to great art treasures of the Renaissance.

1970   A huge tidal wave struck the delta region of East Pakistan killing an estimated 250,000 people; the greatest disaster of modern times.

CLASSIFICATION OF LIVING THINGS

HOW THIS ANIMAL IS CLASSIFIED

In classifying plants and animals, scientists group the plants and animals that are very much alike into species. Species that are much alike are grouped into genera (the plural of genus). Genera are put together to form families, families make up orders, orders make up classes, and classes make up phyla (the plural of phylum). For an even more exact classification, classes may be grouped into subphyla and the subphyla into phyla. There may also be suborders, subgenera, and so on. Subspecies are often called varieties.

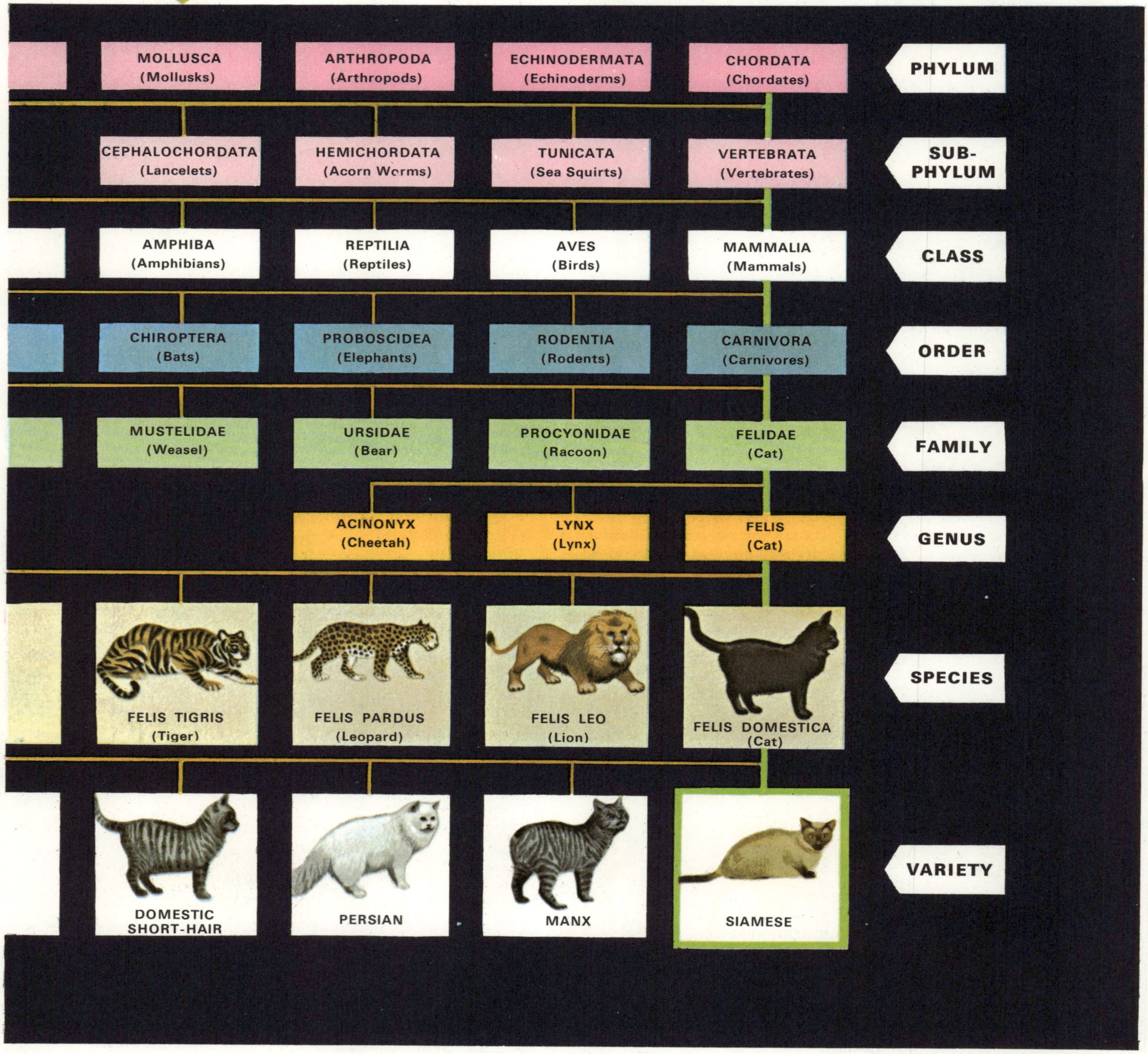

MOLLUSCA (Mollusks)	ARTHROPODA (Arthropods)	ECHINODERMATA (Echinoderms)	CHORDATA (Chordates)	**PHYLUM**
CEPHALOCHORDATA (Lancelets)	HEMICHORDATA (Acorn Worms)	TUNICATA (Sea Squirts)	VERTEBRATA (Vertebrates)	**SUB-PHYLUM**
AMPHIBA (Amphibians)	REPTILIA (Reptiles)	AVES (Birds)	MAMMALIA (Mammals)	**CLASS**
CHIROPTERA (Bats)	PROBOSCIDEA (Elephants)	RODENTIA (Rodents)	CARNIVORA (Carnivores)	**ORDER**
MUSTELIDAE (Weasel)	URSIDAE (Bear)	PROCYONIDAE (Racoon)	FELIDAE (Cat)	**FAMILY**
	ACINONYX (Cheetah)	LYNX (Lynx)	FELIS (Cat)	**GENUS**
FELIS TIGRIS (Tiger)	FELIS PARDUS (Leopard)	FELIS LEO (Lion)	FELIS DOMESTICA (Cat)	**SPECIES**
DOMESTIC SHORT-HAIR	PERSIAN	MANX	SIAMESE	**VARIETY**

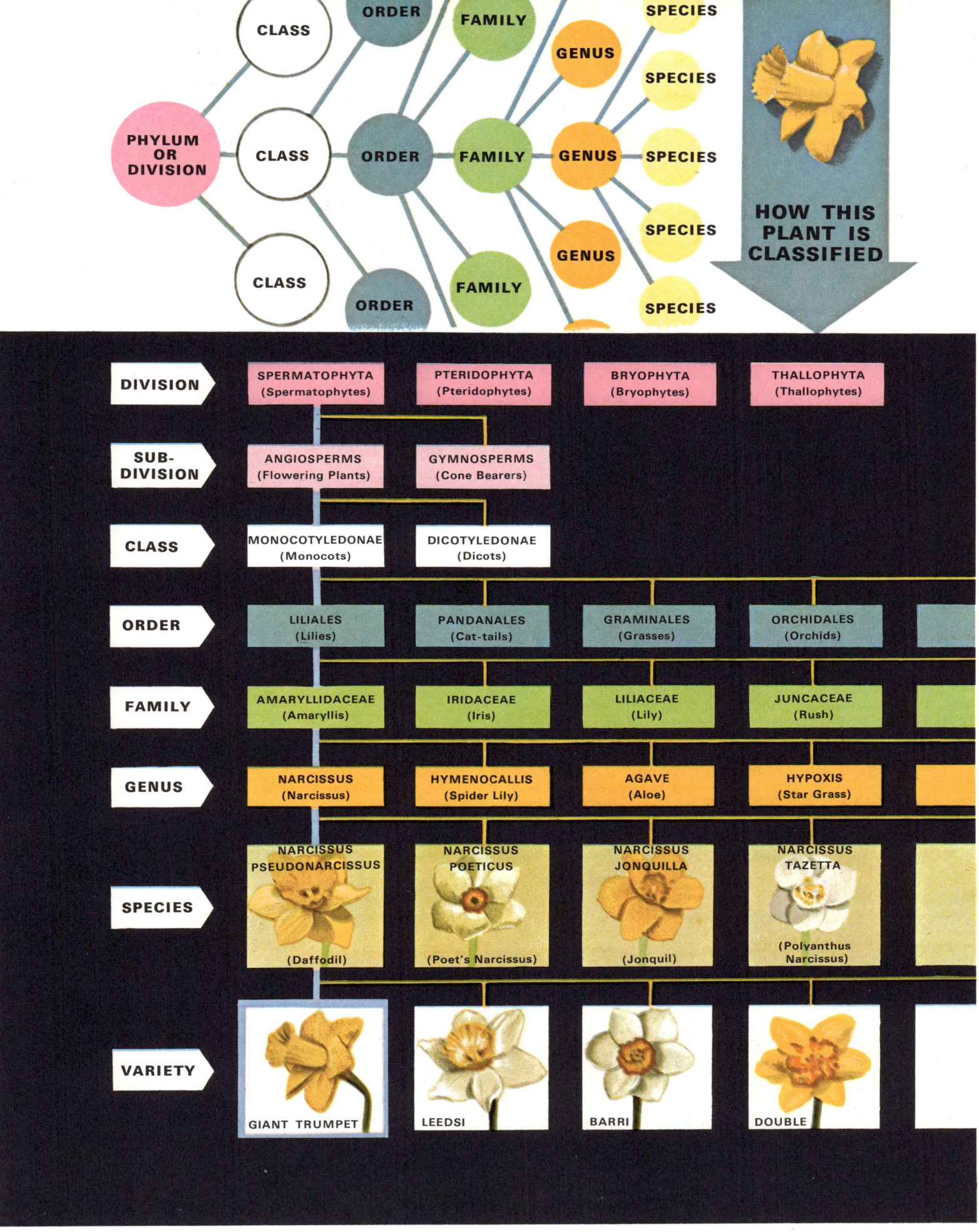

CLASS

ORDER

FAMILY

SPECIES

GENUS

SPECIES

PHYLUM
OR
DIVISION

CLASS

ORDER

FAMILY

GENUS

SPECIES

CLASS

ORDER

FAMILY

GENUS

SPECIES

SPECIES

GENUS

SPECIES

HOW THIS
PLANT IS
CLASSIFIED

DIVISION	SPERMATOPHYTA (Spermatophytes)	PTERIDOPHYTA (Pteridophytes)	BRYOPHYTA (Bryophytes)	THALLOPHYTA (Thallophytes)
SUB-DIVISION	ANGIOSPERMS (Flowering Plants)	GYMNOSPERMS (Cone Bearers)		
CLASS	MONOCOTYLEDONAE (Monocots)	DICOTYLEDONAE (Dicots)		
ORDER	LILIALES (Lilies)	PANDANALES (Cat-tails)	GRAMINALES (Grasses)	ORCHIDALES (Orchids)
FAMILY	AMARYLLIDACEAE (Amaryllis)	IRIDACEAE (Iris)	LILIACEAE (Lily)	JUNCACEAE (Rush)
GENUS	NARCISSUS (Narcissus)	HYMENOCALLIS (Spider Lily)	AGAVE (Aloe)	HYPOXIS (Star Grass)
SPECIES	NARCISSUS PSEUDONARCISSUS (Daffodil)	NARCISSUS POETICUS (Poet's Narcissus)	NARCISSUS JONQUILLA (Jonquil)	NARCISSUS TAZETTA (Polyanthus Narcissus)
VARIETY	GIANT TRUMPET	LEEDSI	BARRI	DOUBLE

51

FOOD PYRAMIDS

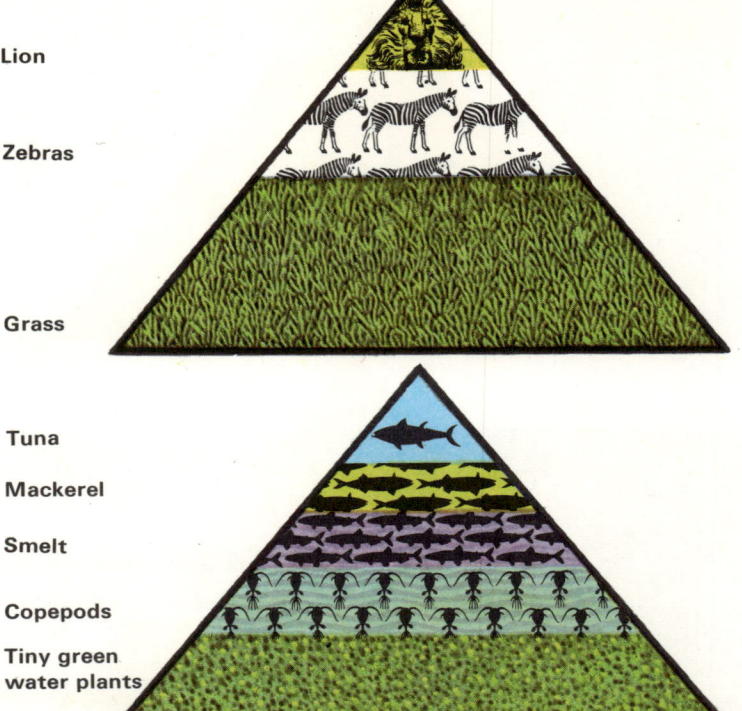

Lion

Zebras

Grass

Tuna

Mackerel

Smelt

Copepods

Tiny green
water plants

Lions eat zebras. Zebras eat grass. Thus the lion, the zebra, and grass make a food chain. It takes a great deal of grass to feed one zebra for a year, and it takes about 20 zebras to feed a lion for a year. This story can be told by a diagram called a food pyramid. The chart at the right shows several food pyramids.

Notice that green plants form the base of each one of these pyramids. The food of every animal can be traced back to green plants. At the top of most pyramids there is a meat-eating (carnivorous) animal.

'LIVING' FOSSILS

Some kinds of plants and animals have lived on, almost unchanged, for millions of years after most or all of their close relatives became extinct. These plants and animals are often called 'living' fossils.

Coelacanth
The fish in the picture is sometimes called a 'living' fossil. Until 1939 scientists thought that all the coelacanths had disappeared about 70 million years ago. But in 1939 a coelacanth was dredged up by a fishing trawler near the tip of South Africa. Since then several other specimens have been found. The coelacanth is a lobefin. It is almost exactly like its ancestors that lived in the last days of the dinosaurs.

Australian Lungfish
The Australian lungfish is another 'living' fossil. For a long time it was known only through its fossils, some of which were found in rocks 200 million years old. But in 1869 living specimens were found

Lingula
Lingula is one of the group of little-known marine animals called brachiopods. It has remained almost exactly the same for about 500 million years. It dates back to the time when there were no animals anywhere with backbones, and when brachiopods were very common and ranked high among the animals of the earth. No other genus of animals has so long a history.

Ginkgo Tree
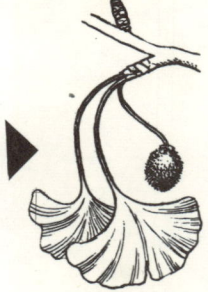
The famous scientist Darwin called attention to this tree as a 'living' fossil. It is the only plant left of a group that flourished in the days of the dinosaurs. The ginkgo is a seed plant, but it is of a primitive kind. Once spread far and wide over the earth, this tree is now found growing wild only in a few places in China.

Peripatus
This worm-like animal does not have any common name, not because it is a newcomer on the earth, but because few people ever see it. It is very much like its ancestors that left their traces in rocks formed 500 million years ago. It has been called 'the worm that didn't turn—into anything.' Peripatus has never been found north of the tropics.

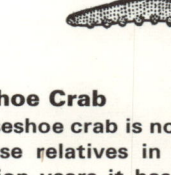

Horseshoe Crab
The horseshoe crab is not a true crab. It has no very close relatives in the world today. For 200 million years it has been able to hold its own with practically no physical change.

52

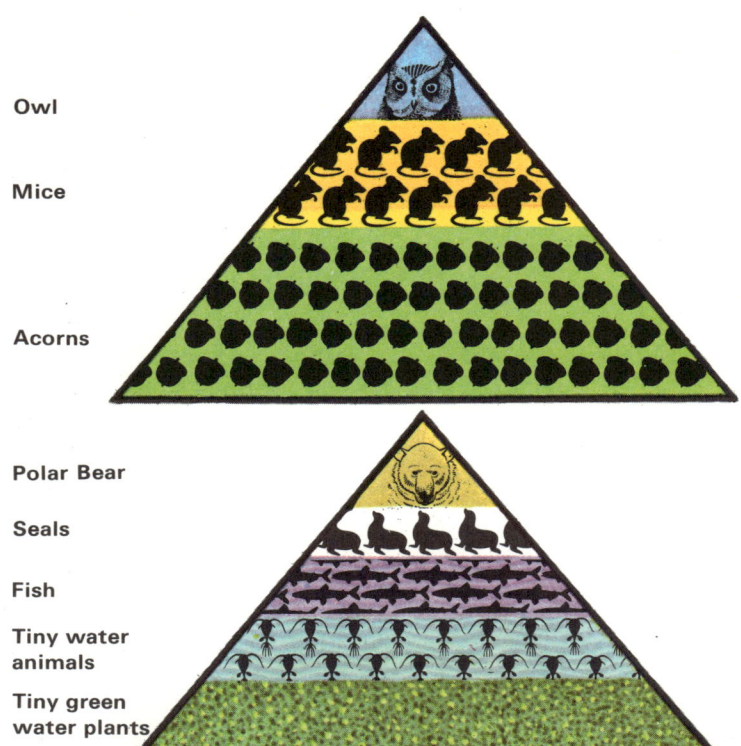

Owl

Mice

Acorns

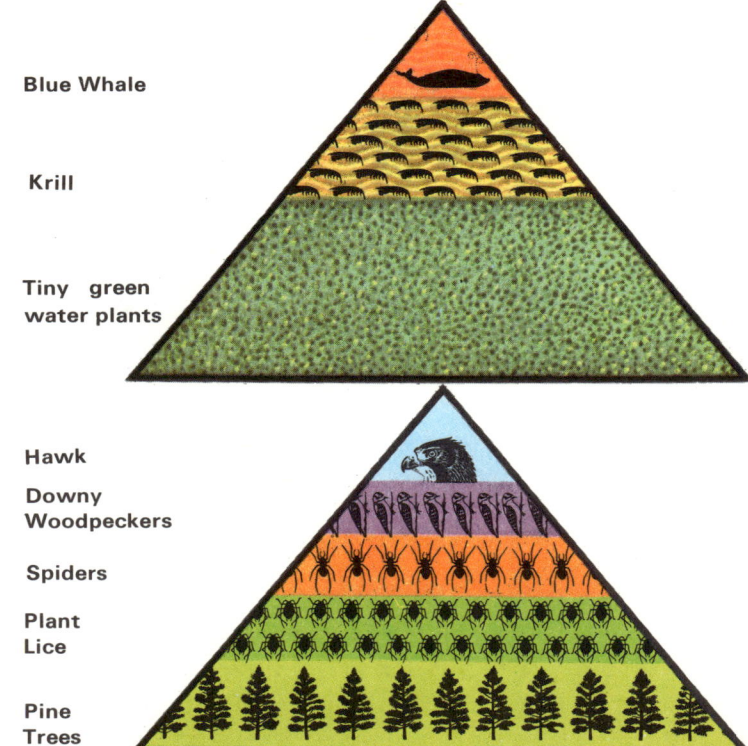

Blue Whale

Krill

Tiny green water plants

Polar Bear

Seals

Fish

Tiny water animals

Tiny green water plants

Hawk

Downy Woodpeckers

Spiders

Plant Lice

Pine Trees

Sequoias
The first sequoia-like trees appeared more than 100 million years ago, during the Age of Reptiles. They were very successful. In time there were many species of sequoias, probably more than a hundred, and they formed great forests in Europe and Asia as well as in the Americas. They were the lords of the plant world. But now only two kinds of sequoias are left—the big tree and the coast redwood—and they are found only in small areas near the western coast of the United States. The metasequoia, a closely-related tree, is another 'living' fossil. It was long believed to be extinct but was recently discovered in central China. Its common name is dawn redwood.

Tuatara
This small reptile has remained almost unchanged for more than 200 million years. During its long history on the earth its relatives the dinosaurs, pterosaurs, ichthyosaurs, and plesiosaurs appeared, became the earth's leading animals, and then completely died out. Today the tuatara is found only on some small islands near New Zealand.

Okapi
The okapi deserves the name of 'living' fossil because it is almost exactly like its ancestors of 30 million years ago. It has no close relatives, but its nearest relative is the giraffe.

Welwitschia
This queer plant is another holdover from nature's early experiments with seed plants. It is quite unlike any other plant in the world. There are only two other plants that are at all closely related, and they do not look like welwitschia. This 'living' fossil from long ago grows only in south-western Africa.

FLOWER PARTS

Complete flowers have parts of four kinds. These parts are called pistils, stamens, petals and sepals.

The pistils contain ovules which, when fertilised by means of pollen, become seeds. The part of a pistil containing the ovules is the *ovary*. Above the ovary is the *style*. The style has at some place, usually its top, a sticky surface called a *stigma*. The stigma serves to hold in place the pollen that reaches it.

Each stamen ends in an *anther,* or pollen sac, in which pollen is formed. The stalk of a stamen is its *filament*.

The petals surround the stamens and pistils. As a rule they form the showy part of the flower. The petals together make up the *corolla*.

The sepals are outside the petals and in many cases form a protective covering when the flower is in bud. The sepals together make up the *calyx*.

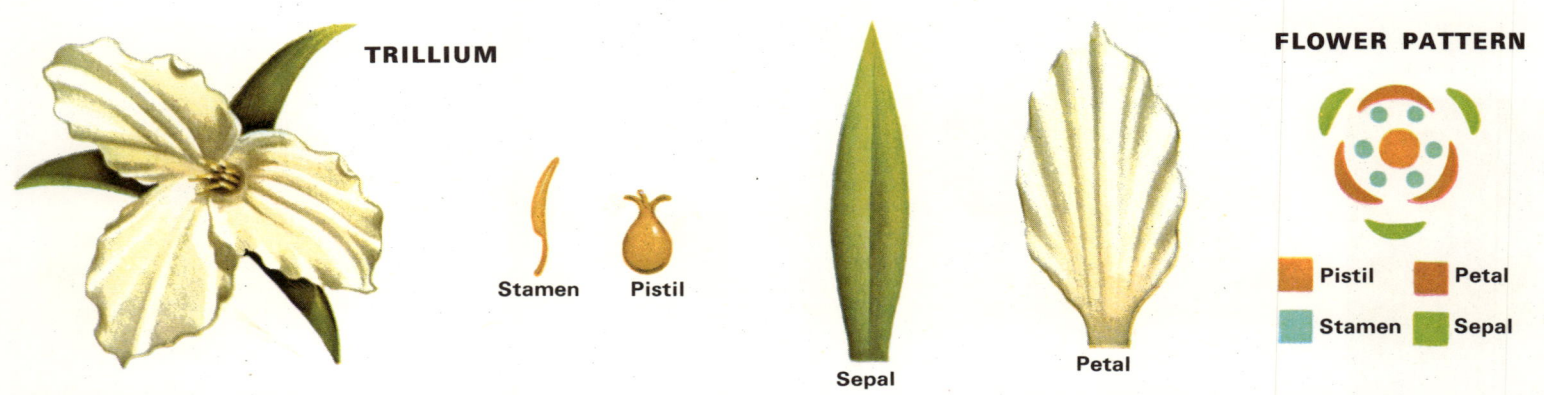

TRILLIUM

Stamen   Pistil

Sepal   Petal

FLOWER PATTERN

Pistil   Petal
Stamen   Sepal

TYPES OF FLOWERS

MORNING-GLORY
In the morning-glory the petals are joined together. Such flowers are sympetalous.

TULIP AND IRIS
In some flowers, such as the tulip and the iris, the sepals are as pretty as the petals. They can be told from the petals because they are outside the petals.

Staminate flower   Pistillate flower

WILLOW
Willows have two kinds of flowers. One kind has a petal but no stamens; the other stamens but no pistil. In most cases the two kinds are on different plants. Most willows are therefore said to be dioecious (two households). Each willow flower is protected by a little leaf called a bract.

POINSETTIA
What appears to be a big flower on a poinsettia is really a group of small flowers surrounded by a circle of showy, coloured leaves.

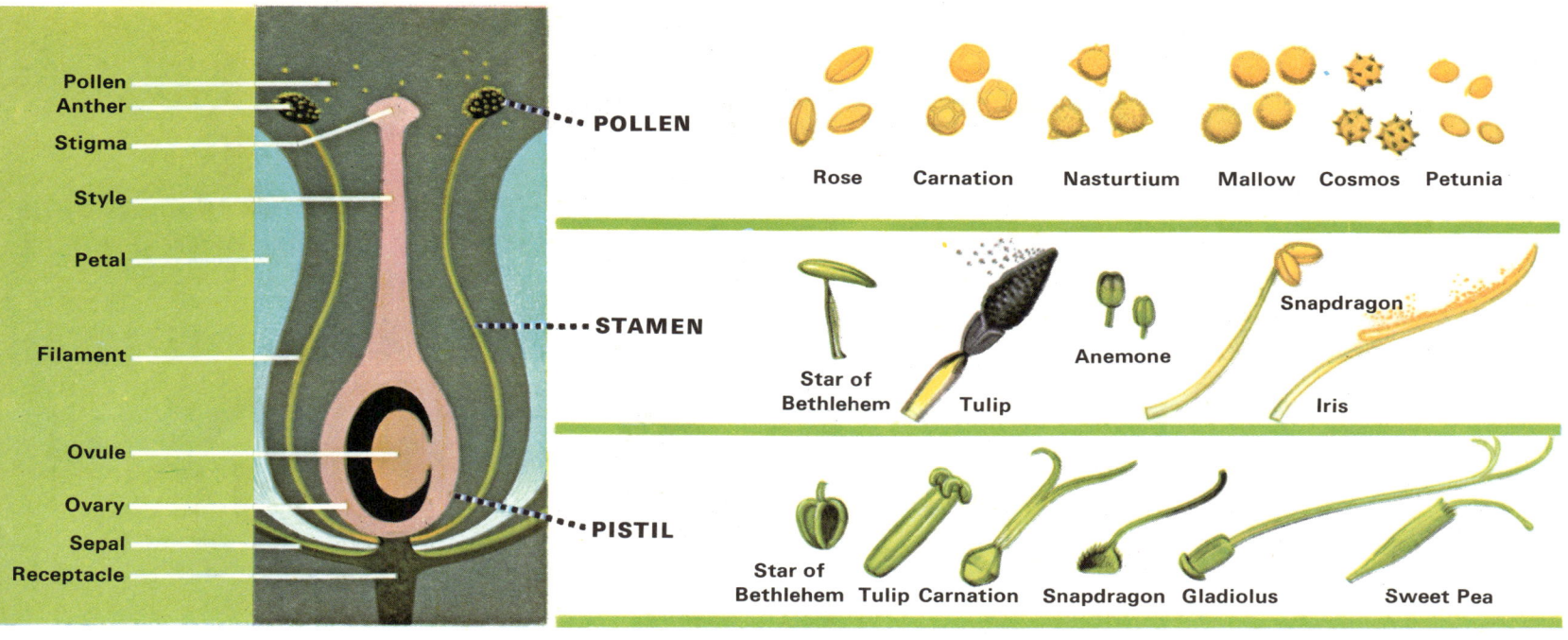

Pollen
Anther
Stigma

Style

Petal

Filament

Ovule

Ovary

Sepal
Receptacle

POLLEN

STAMEN

PISTIL

Rose   Carnation   Nasturtium   Mallow   Cosmos   Petunia

Star of
Bethlehem   Tulip   Anemone   Snapdragon   Iris

Star of
Bethlehem   Tulip   Carnation   Snapdragon   Gladiolus   Sweet Pea

FLOWER PATTERN

Pistil   Petal
Stamen   Sepal

Petal

Stamen   Pistil   Sepal

PANSY

PUMPKIN

Pumpkin vines have two kinds of flowers, one with a pistil and the other with stamens. But both kinds of flowers occur on the same vine. A pumpkin, therefore, is said to be monoecious (one household). Only the pistillate flowers produce the actual orange-coloured pumpkin.

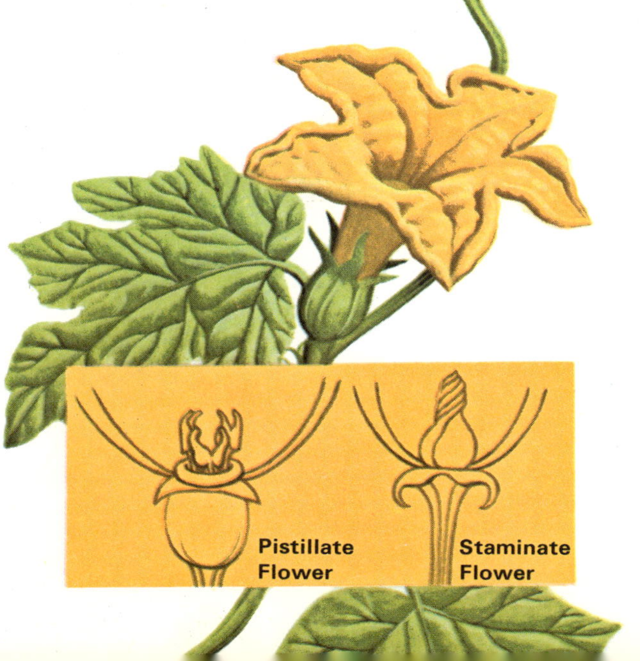

Pistillate
Flower   Staminate
Flower

RED CLOVER, DANDELION, DAISY

Some 'flowers' are whole bouquets of tiny flowers. In some cases all the flowers of the bouquet are alike; in others they are not.

Disc Flower   Ray Flower

Daisy

Red Clover Flower   Dandelion Flower

Dandelion

Red Clover

55

SOME FAMILIES OF FLOWERING PLANTS

After flowering plants first appeared some 130 million years ago, they rapidly 'took the earth.' Now there are more kinds of flowering plants than all other plants put together. There are perhaps as many as 200,000 species. They belong in several hundred plant families. In some of the families there are hundreds of species; in others there are only a few.

Scientists study chiefly the flowers of a flowering plant to find out what other flowering plants it is related to. Without a study of their flowers it is hard to see why, for example, the wild rose and the apple belong in the same family or why the onion and the Easter lily are cousins. This chart names some of the many families of flowering plants and shows a few of the plants that belong in those families.

MALLOW (Malvaceae) 1,000 species

COTTON

HOLLYHOCK

HIBISCUS

ROSE OF SHARON

OKRA

MADDER (Rubiaceae) 5,000 species

BUTTONBUSH   WOODRUFF   BEDSTRAW

PARTRIDGE BERRY   COFFEE

VIOLET (Violaceae) 300 species

VIOLET

PANSY

FEN VIOLET

HEATH (Ericaceae) 1,400 species

HEATHER

AZALEA

RHODODENDRON

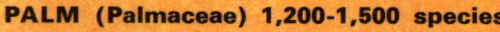
PALM (Palmaceae) 1,200-1,500 species

PALMETTO

COCONUT PALM

ROYAL PALM

DATE PALM

ROSE (Rosaceae) 2,500 species

ROSE BLACKBERRY RASPBERRY CINQUEFOIL MOUNTAIN ASH

APPLE CHERRY PEAR PLUM PEACH APRICOT

CRAB APPLE ALMOND QUINCE HAWTHORN STRAWBERRY

MORNING GLORY (Convolvulaceae) 1,000 species

MORNING-GLORY

BINDWEED

SWEET POTATO

DODDER

RUE (Rutaceae) 900 species

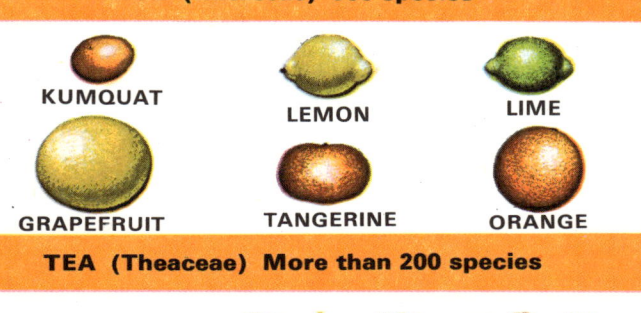

KUMQUAT LEMON LIME

GRAPEFRUIT TANGERINE ORANGE

TEA (Theaceae) More than 200 species

TEA FRANKLINIA TREE CAMELLIA

GRASS (Poaceae) 7,000 species

SORGHUM TIMOTHY RICE FOXTAIL GRASS BARLEY

OATS BAMBOO SUGAR CANE

MAIZE WHEAT BROOMCORN RYE MILLET

PEA (Leguminosae) 12,000 species

GARDEN PEA COWPEA SNAP BEAN SOYA BEAN

LENTIL LIMA BEAN SWEET PEA

RED CLOVER PEANUT LUPINE LUCERNE

VETCH REDBUD BROOM CAROB TREE

NIGHTSHADE (Solanaceae) 1,700 species

AUBERGINE

BITTERSWEET

PETUNIA

NIGHTSHADE

PEPPER

GROUND CHERRY

TOMATO

JERUSALEM CHERRY

POTATO

TOBACCO

GOURD (Cucurbitaceae) 700 species

CANTALOUPE   HONEYDEW MELON   SQUASH   WATERMELON   GOURD   CUCUMBER   PUMPKIN

OLIVE (Oleanceae) 500 species

BUTTERCUP (Ranunculaceae) 1,200 species

FORSYTHIA

PASQUE FLOWER   CLEMATIS   PEONY   COLUMBINE   BUTTERCUP

MONKSHOOD   LARKSPUR   BANEBERRY   HEPATICA   MEADOW RUE

PRIVET   LILAC

ORCHID (Orchidaceae) 5,000-10,000 species

MOCCASIN FLOWER   ORCHID   SHOWY LADY'S-SLIPPER

ASH TREE

COMPOSITE (Compositae) 13,000-20,000 species

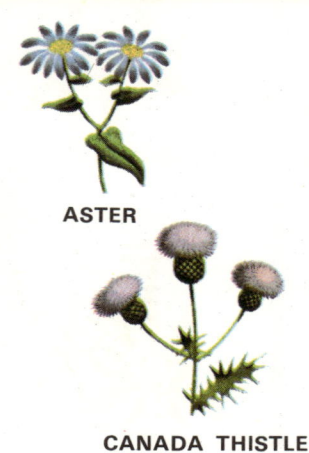

OLIVE

ASTER

DAISY

SUNFLOWER

CANADA THISTLE

LETTUCE

MARIGOLD

58

MUSTARD (Cruciferae) 2,000 species

CABBAGE · BRUSSELS-SPROUTS · KOHL RABI · RADISH · TURNIP · STOCK · WATERCRESS

MUSTARD · RAPE · SWEET ALYSSUM · KALE · HORSERADISH · PEPPERGRASS

PARSLEY (Umbelliferae) 2,500 species

CARROT · PARSNIP · CELERY · CORN CARAWAY · QUEEN ANNE'S LACE · POISON HEMLOCK · PARSLEY

LILY (Lilaceae) 12,500 species

GARLIC · ONION · LILY-OF-THE-VALLEY · TULIP · TRILLIUM · HYACINTH

TIGER LILY · DOG'S TOOTH VIOLET · EASTER LILY · DAY LILY · YUCCA · ASPARAGUS

LAUREL (Lauraceae) 1,100 species

SASSAFRAS

SPICE BUSH

LAUREL

CINNAMON TREE

AVOCADO, OR ALLIGATOR PEAR

MINT (Labiatae) 3,000 species

SPEAR-MINT · PEPPERMINT · THYME · HOREHOUND · CATMINT · SAGE · SELF-HEAL · LAVENDER

GOLDENROD · DANDELION · BACHELOR'S BUTTON

ZINNIA · COSMOS · RAGWEED

59

Starfish
(Asterias)

Egg ribbon of
the Giant Whelk

Sea-potato

SNAILS
AND SHELLS

Garden Snail
(Helix hortensis)

Edible Snail
(Helix pomatia)

Most of the shells we find on the sea-shore are empty, but they were all once the homes of snails, shellfish and other animals without backbones which lived on the coast. Good examples of similar land animals are the garden snail, the slug, and the edible snail, which grows to a length of about 3 or 4 inches and has a shell $1\frac{1}{2}$ to 2 inches high.

The snail's shell is all in one piece, coiled round a single cavity. A mussel, on the other hand, has two cavities. The mussel can open and close both of its halves. Hundreds of different kinds of sea animals resemble the mussel when they make their homes and many also resemble the snail.

Most sea animals make their own shells, more often than not from the chalk in the water. After a tea kettle has been in use for a certain length of time, chalk is deposited on the inside surfaces. Sea creatures make their shells out of exactly the same substance.

One kind of animal is often found inside shells which it has borrowed from other creatures—the hermit crab usually lives in empty winkle shells.

Many shells have names which give us some idea what they look like: 'Bleeding Tooth', 'Slipper' and 'Razor' are some of them.

Often the shells of the same kind of animal come in different colours. That is why it is so interesting to collect butterfly shells. One can find them in so many different colours. The same is true of scallop shells.

Sun-dial Shell
(Solarium)

Scallop Shell with barnacles
(Balanus)

Conch Shell (Strombus)

Butterfly Shell
(Donax)

Auger Shell
(Terebra)

'Bleeding Tooth' (Nerita)

Scallop Shell
(Pecten)

Razor Shell
(Solen)

Band Shell
(Fasciolaria)

Cone Shell
(Conus)

Giant Whelk (Busycon)

Gibbula
(Trochus)

Cockle
(Cardium)

Slipper Limpet
(Crepidula)

Piddock Shell
(Pholas)

Cowry Shell
(Cyprea)

Ark Shell (Arca)

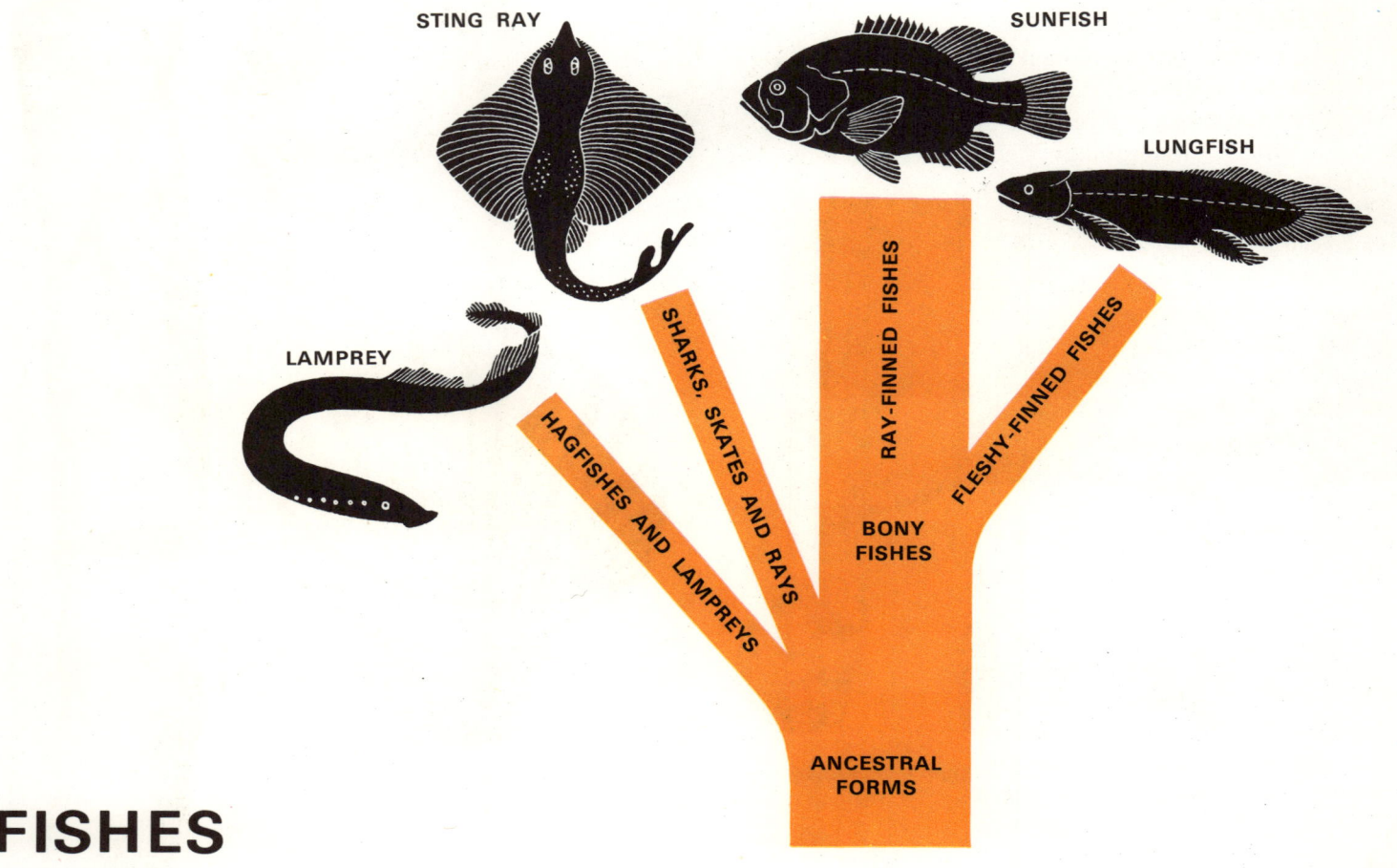

STING RAY

SUNFISH

LUNGFISH

LAMPREY

SHARKS, SKATES AND RAYS

RAY-FINNED FISHES

FLESHY-FINNED FISHES

HAGFISHES AND LAMPREYS

BONY FISHES

ANCESTRAL FORMS

FISHES

FISH FACTS

Fishes are vertebrates, but some have skeletons of cartilage rather than of bone.

Fishes are cold-blooded.

All fishes have gills: lungfishes have lungs in addition to gills.

All true fishes have fins. Many have two pairs which correspond to our arms and legs.

Most fishes are covered with scales when fully grown.

Rings in the scales of a fish tell the fish's age just as rings in the wood of a tree trunk tell the age of the tree.

Fishes swim chiefly by moving their tails and tail fins from side to side. Their other fins help in steering and balancing.

Many fishes have a swim bladder filled with air. Changing the amount of air in its swim bladder helps a fish go up or down in the water.

A fish's heart has only two chambers.

Most fishes hatch from eggs, but some are live-bearing.

All fishes live in water; some live in salt water, some live in fresh water, and some spend part of their lives in fresh water and part in salt water.

Although all fishes are water animals, some, especially the lungfishes, have ways of surviving when the streams and ponds in which they live dry up.

Fishes have no external ears. Their internal ears are deep within their brain cases.

Some ray-finned fishes are called spiny rayed fishes because they have spines supporting their fins. The perch is a typical spiny rayed fish.

Fishes cannot close their eyes; they have no eyelids.

With the sense organs along its lateral line, a fish can sense movement and changes in pressure in the water surrounding it.

Many fishes make noises—drones, croaks, grunts, cackles, squawks, purrs, and other sounds. Fish noises can be picked up with a hydrophone.

Some fishes live in very cold water. Scientists have blasted holes in Antarctic ice to collect fishes from the water under the ice.

The food of most fishes can be traced back to diatoms, microscopic green plants.

The first fishes appeared on the earth long before any other animals with backbones.

Many of the fishes of past ages had armour.

FISH FIGURES

Fishes form the largest group of backboned animals. There are at least 20,000 species.

The ling, or mud hake, is a relative of the common cod. This fish is famous for the number of eggs it lays—about 28 million at a time. But fewer than one in a million hatch and live.

A kind of goby found in the Philippines is one of the smallest, if not the very smallest, fish in the world. It is less than half an inch long when full grown.

The whale shark is the largest of all fishes. A whale shark may be 45 feet long and weigh 50 tons. Some sharks are man-eaters, but the whale shark is harmless. It eats very small animals, called plankton, which it strains from the sea water it swims in.

One of the most common fishes in the sea is one which a great many people have never seen or even heard of. It is a deep-water fish called the bristlemouth.

Less than $\frac{1}{50}$ of all the kinds of fishes known in the world are now being used as food, for their oil, or as fertiliser.

In the United States the total annual fish 'harvest' amounts to about one million pounds.

The total annual catch of fish in the whole world is about 30 million tons. More than 95 per cent of this catch is made in the waters of the northern hemisphere.

Herring, like many other fishes, swim in schools or shoals. One shoal of herring is likely to have from 3,000 million herrings in it. About 10,000 million are caught every year. The herring is considered the world's most important food fish.

The fish who live half a mile down in the ocean stand a

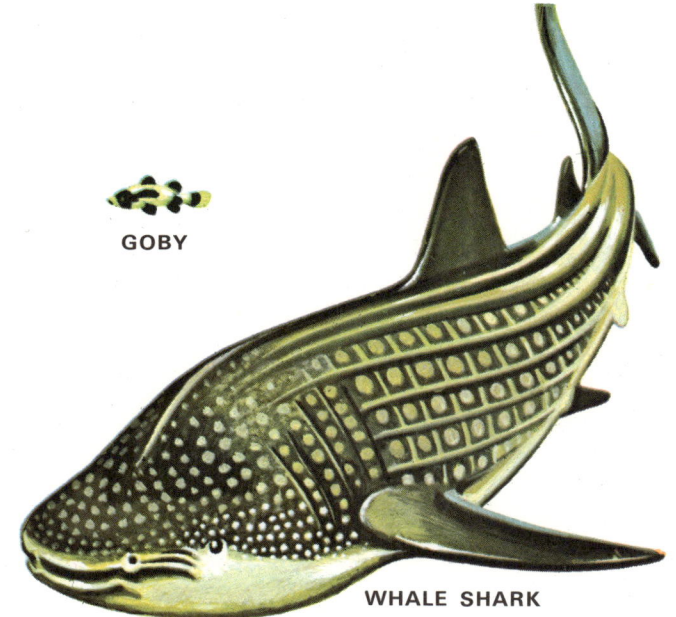

GOBY

WHALE SHARK

pressure of more than 1,000 pounds on every square inch of their bodies.

A species of fish can hold its own if only two of the off-spring of every female fish survive.

Some fishes make journeys of thousands of miles. The eel is one, the salmon is another.

Some fishes are very fast swimmers. The blue marlin can swim at 50 miles an hour—faster than a horse can run. There are even faster fishes—for example, the swordfish and the sailfish.

There have been fishes on the earth for a period of at least 400 million years.

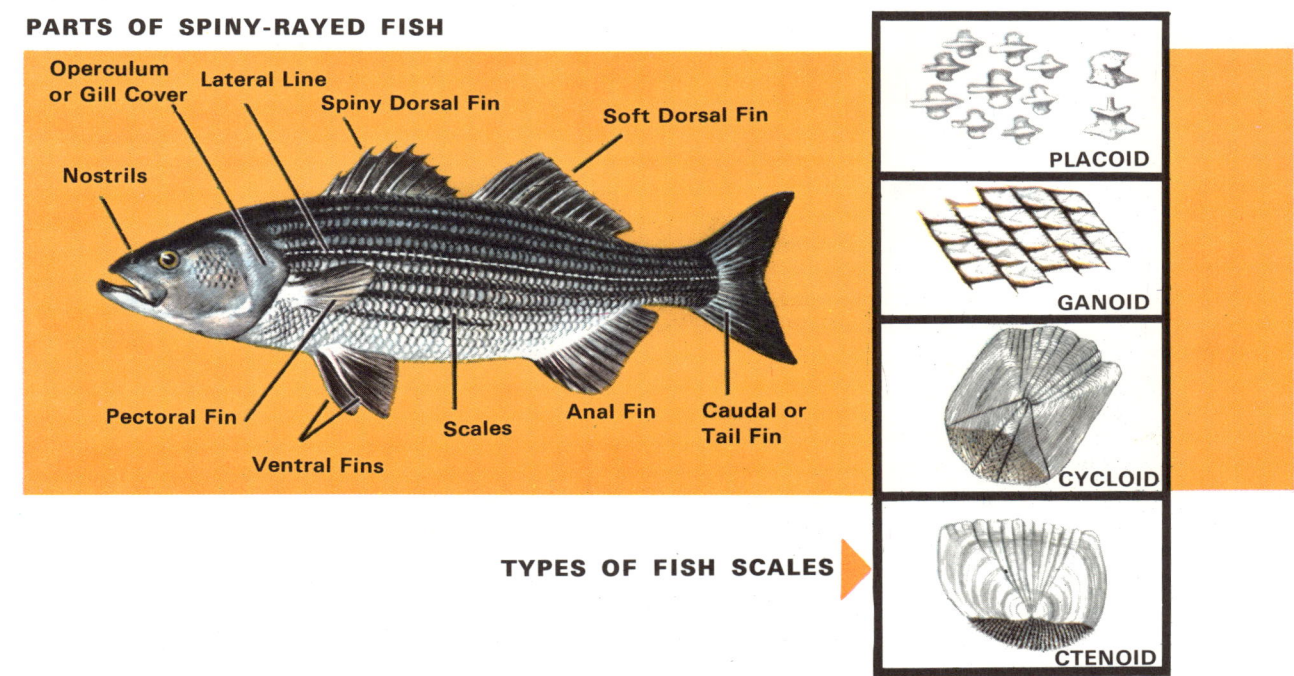

PARTS OF SPINY-RAYED FISH

Operculum or Gill Cover
Lateral Line
Spiny Dorsal Fin
Soft Dorsal Fin
Nostrils
Pectoral Fin
Ventral Fins
Scales
Anal Fin
Caudal or Tail Fin

PLACOID
GANOID
CYCLOID
CTENOID

TYPES OF FISH SCALES ▶

SEA HORSE

FLYING FISH

SOME UNUSUAL FISH

ARCHER FISH

BLACK SWALLOWER

CLIMBING PERCH

SEA HORSE. The little sea horse often swims head-up in a very un-fishlike way. The male sea horse has a pouch on its underside in which it carries the eggs the female lays, until they hatch.

ARCHER FISH. The little archer fish of Asia gets its name from the strange way in which it catches its food. It 'shoots' the insects it eats. Its arrow is a stream of water which it shoots out of its mouth.

BLACK SWALLOWER. The black swallower is a tiny deep-sea fish. This fish eats other fish, and often swallows a fish much bigger than itself. Both its mouth and its stomach can stretch enormously.

CLIMBING PERCH. A climbing perch is not as 'lost' out of water as a fish is supposed to be. This little fish of Asia has a way of holding water around its gills so that it can stay out of water for some time.

SWORDFISH. A full-grown swordfish may weigh 1,100 pounds and be 15 feet long. The sword which gives this fish its name may be more than a yard long and strong enough to pierce a small boat.

SAILFISH. The sailfish has a sword, but this fish is much smaller than a swordfish. Not many sailfishes weigh more than 200 pounds. The sailfish is one of the fastest fishes, and one of the most beautiful.

OCEAN SUNFISH. The ocean sunfish is often called the headfish, for it is almost all head. A full-grown headfish may weigh up to 2,000 pounds. As one would guess from its shape, the ocean sunfish is not at all a fast swimmer.

ELECTRIC EEL. Several fishes can give electric shocks to any enemy attacking them. The fish that gives the most powerful shocks to its enemies is the electric eel of South America. Its shock can stun a horse.

ANGLER. Anglers get their name from the 'fishing rods' they carry around on their heads. The angler pictured lives in the deep sea. The 'bait' on its fishing rod is luminous.

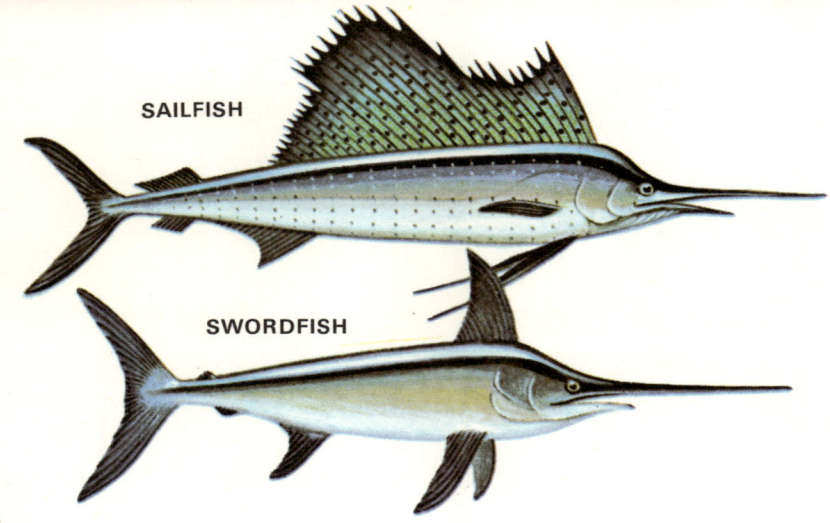
SAILFISH

SWORDFISH

OCEAN SUNFISH

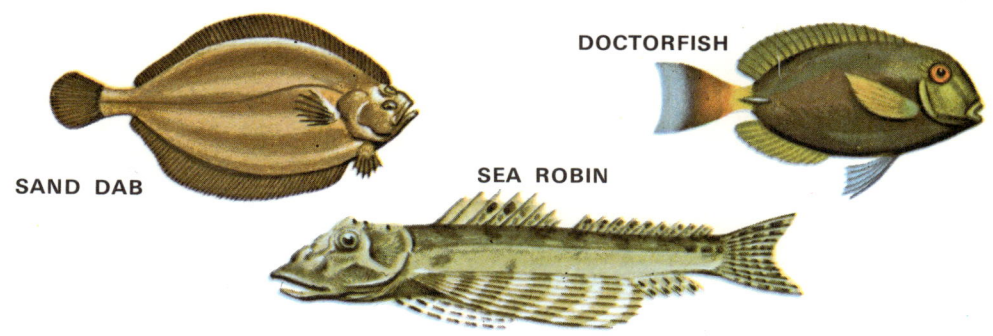
SAND DAB

DOCTORFISH

SEA ROBIN

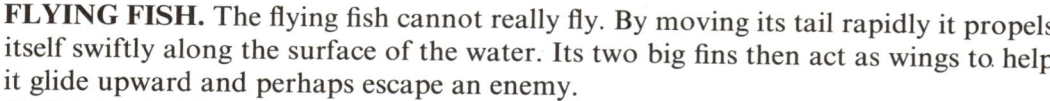

CLOWN FISH

STICKLEBACK

MUDSKIPPER

PIRANHA

FOUR-EYES

FLYING FISH. The flying fish cannot really fly. By moving its tail rapidly it propels itself swiftly along the surface of the water. Its two big fins then act as wings to help it glide upward and perhaps escape an enemy.

SAND DAB. The sand dab is a flatfish. All the flatfishes swim about and lie on the ocean floor on their sides. Both their eyes are on the side that is uppermost. The sand dab is so thin that light can shine through it.

SEA ROBIN. The sea robin is sometimes called the 'walking fish.' Its 'legs,' which are a part of its pectoral fins, serve as feelers for finding food on the sea bed. It finds worms and shellfish there.

DOCTORFISH. The doctorfish, or common surgeon, gets its name from two spines that are as sharp as a doctor's lancet. These two spines are on the fish's sides just in front of its tail.

CLOWN FISH. The clown fish has formed a partnership with certain kinds of sea anemones. The sea anemones, with their stinging cells, protect the fish from its enemies. In exchange for this protection the clown fish brings food to the anemones.

STICKLEBACK. Most egg-laying fishes deposit their eggs and then leave them. But some fishes build nests for their eggs and guard the nests. The small stickleback is one of the nest-building fishes.

MUDSKIPPER. This little fish, which lives along the shores of West Africa, spends much time perching on rocks or tree roots at the edge of the water. It can walk, run, and even jump with its fins and tail.

PIRANHA. This fish of the Amazon River has teeth that can bite into steel. It has the reputation of being one of the fiercest of all fishes. Another name for the piranha is 'tiger fish.'

FOUR-EYES. The four-eyes gets its name from the fact that each of its eyes is divided into two parts. As the fish swims along the surface, the upper parts of its eyes see above the surface, the lower parts see below it.

PORCUPINE FISH. The spines of the porcupine fish serve to protect it from its enemies. A porcupine fish, moreover, can puff itself up so that it is too big for some of its enemies to swallow.

ELECTRIC EEL

PORCUPINE FISH

ANGLER

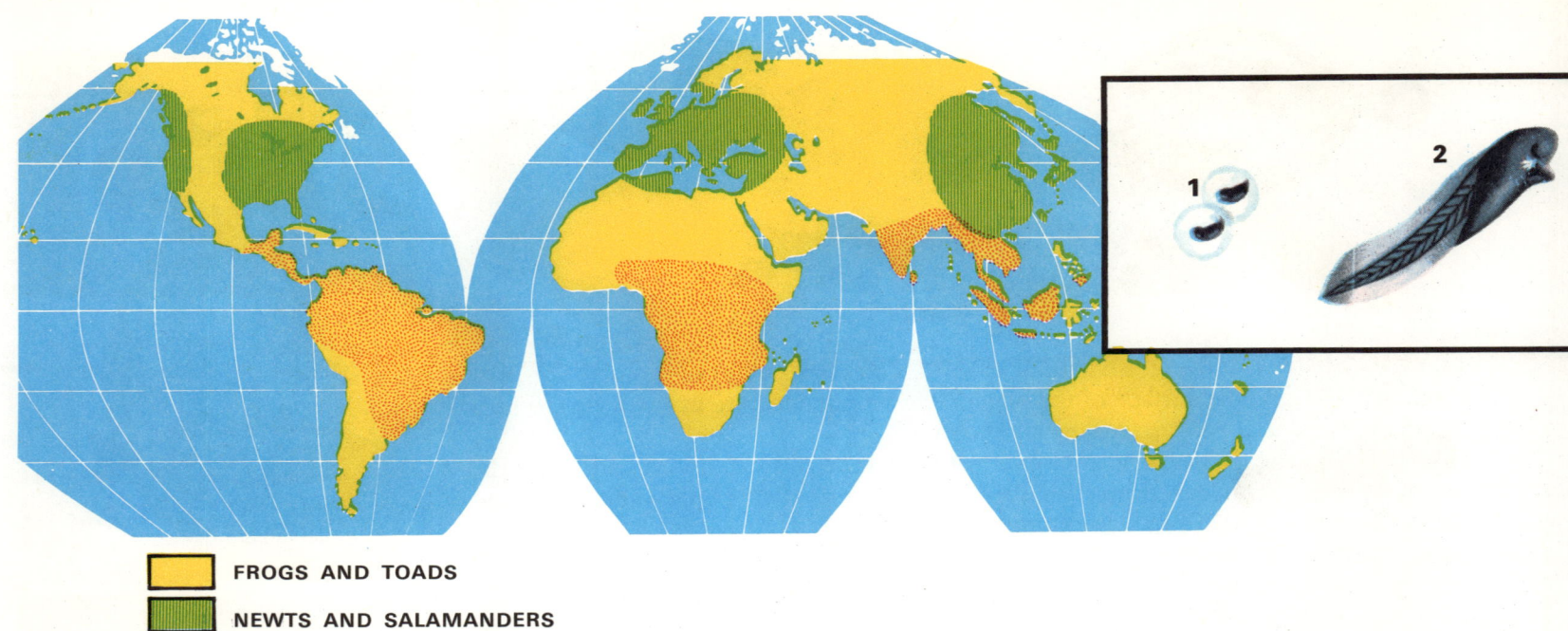

FROGS AND TOADS

NEWTS AND SALAMANDERS

CAECILIANS

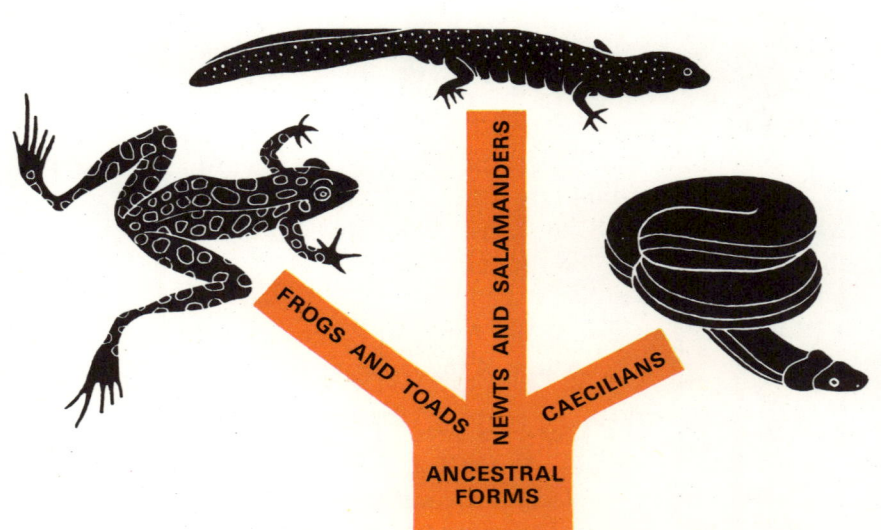

AMPHIBIANS

Amphibians are vertebrates; they all have backbones. They have no scales, fur or feathers; their skins are bare.

Like all animals except birds and mammals, amphibians are cold-blooded. Those that live in regions with cold winters hibernate.

'Amphibian' means 'living in two places.' As a rule, amphibians live in water and breathe with gills when young. When grown most of them live on land and breathe with lungs or through their skin. Some, like the western axolotl, rarely grow up to be air-breathing creatures.

There are about 2,000 species of amphibians. Of these about 60 are caecilians, about 200 are newts or salamanders, and the rest are toads or frogs.

Newts and salamanders have both legs and tails when grown. Toads and frogs have legs but no tails when fully

grown. Caecilians have no legs and only very short tails.

There are no amphibians, young or old, in the sea.

Almost all amphibians hatch from eggs; only one kind is known to be born alive—a rare African frog named *Nectophrynoides*.

Many amphibians change greatly in appearance as they grow up. Young toads and frogs are called tadpoles. Young amphibians of other kinds are usually called larvae.

Amphibians must have moist surroundings. There is no truth to the old belief that a salamander could live in a blazing fire.

The largest amphibian is the five-foot long giant salamander of Japan. The smallest amphibians are the tree frogs.

The earliest four-legged animals were amphibians. Amphibians were the first animals to have voices.

Life History of a Typical Amphibian, a Frog

'FISHES THAT WALKED'

The amphibians are descendants of the fishes. The first amphibians may be spoken of as 'fishes that walked.' Scientists believe that the move from water to land came about in some such way as this: long dry periods made life difficult for the fish in ponds and streams and shallow seas. The water became foul, and it was hard for the fish to get enough oxygen. The simple lungs which some fishes of the time had were a big help. To escape from the foul water for a little while, the fishes with lungs would flop up on land and breathe with their lungs. Of course, their fins were not good for land travel. But generation by generation, their fins grew stouter until finally they were stubby legs. At the same time their lungs grew better. The creatures lost many of their fish characteristics and were air-breathing animals that could live a large part of their lives on land; they were amphibians.

A GIANT AMPHIBIAN OF LONG AGO

Millions of years ago there were amphibians much larger than any amphibians of today. One of these big amphibians was *Eryops*. *Eryops* was over 8 feet long and had a head 18 inches across. Its mouth was enormous. Scientists believe from the fossils of this ancient amphibian that *Eryops*, like many of its relatives, had three eyes—two in the usual place and one in the top of its head.

The legs of *Eryops* were very short; they did not hold the creature far above the ground. Probably it spent most of its time sunning itself near the edge of a swamp or pond and waiting for a fish to be washed up on shore or for a smaller amphibian or a reptile to come close enough to be caught. Probably *Eryops* ate some insects, too; many big insects existed at that time. The picture of *Eryops* shows that it looked much like crocodiles look today.

THE PUZZLING AXOLOTL

'Axolotl' is an Aztec word meaning 'servant of the water.' The name was given long ago to a salamander found in mountain lakes of Mexico and western United States. As the people who gave it a name knew it, this creature never grew up. Even though it produced young, it kept its larval shape and its gills and continued to live in water. Now scientists have found that the axolotl is merely the larval form of the tiger salamander. In the eastern part of the United States this salamander follows the usual salamander pattern of spending its early life in water and its later life as an air-breathing animal on land. Scientists have found that occasionally a western axolotl will follow this pattern. Why the life-histories, as a rule, differ in the different regions is puzzling.

ERYOPS

REPTILES OF TODAY

There are at least five thousand kinds of reptiles living now.

Reptiles are vertebrates; they have back-bones. Like fishes, amphibians, and all invertebrates, they are cold blooded.

Reptiles breathe with lungs all their lives. They do not at any time breathe with gills. Every cold-blooded animal that has a back-bone but never has gills is a reptile.

The word 'reptile' means 'crawling animal.' But not all reptiles crawl, and not all animals that crawl are reptiles.

Different groups of reptiles differ greatly in appearance. Turtles have legs and shells; alligators and crocodiles have legs but no shells; snakes have no legs and no shells. Most lizards have legs, but a few do not. None of them have shells.

The tuatara looks much like a lizard, but it differs from the lizards enough to make scientists put it in an order all by itself.

The tuatara has the longest history of any reptile living today. It has been on the earth in almost the same form for more than 200 million years. Now it is found only on islands near New Zealand. It grows to be about two feet long.

Reptiles, with very few exceptions, are covered with scales. Contrary to the belief of most people, they are not slimy.

By far the greatest number of reptiles are land animals; even those that live in water come out onto land to lay their eggs.

Most reptiles lay eggs, but some snakes and lizards carry their eggs inside their bodies until the young snakes develop. The little reptiles are then born alive.

Reptiles are far more common in warm regions than in those with cold winters. The snakes and lizards found in regions of cold winters must hibernate.

All alligators, crocodiles, and snakes are meat eaters. The tuatara is a meat eater, too; it chiefly eats insects. Most lizards are meat eaters, but some are vegetarians. Turtles eat both plant and animal food.

Snakes have immovable eyelids. They have forked tongues; so do some lizards.

Turtles have no teeth.

Today reptiles rank in number of species far below the fishes, birds and mammals of today.

Era	Period	SNAKES	LIZARDS	CROCODILES	TURTLES	TUATARA
CENOZOIC	TERTIARY (70 million years)					
MESOZOIC	CRETACEOUS (60 million years)					
	JURASSIC (35 million years)					
	TRIASSIC (35 million years)					
PALAEOZOIC	PERMIAN (30 million years)					

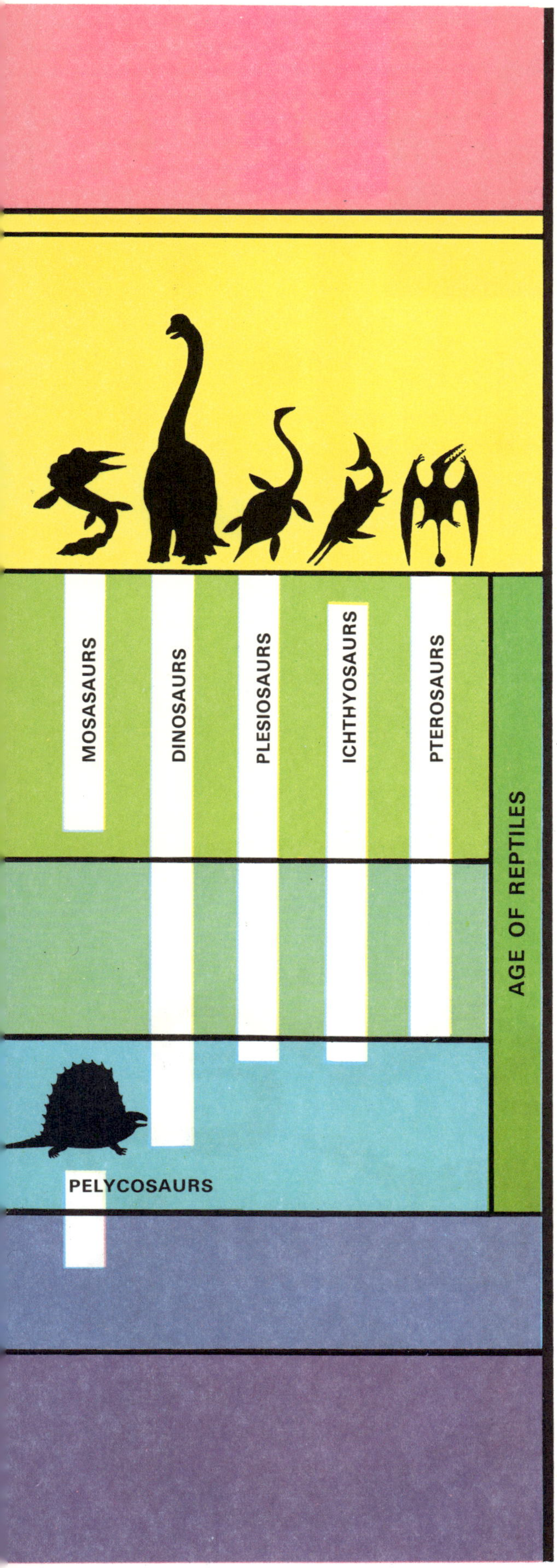

REPTILES OF LONG AGO

For many millions of years reptiles were the earth's leading animals. That time is called the Age of Reptiles. Several groups of reptiles that were very common then are extinct today.

Among the early reptiles were the *pelycosaurs*. Some of them had great 'sails' growing upward from their backs. In spite of their sails, these reptiles lived on land.

The *plesiosaurs* were reptiles of the sea. A plesiosaur had a broad, rather flat body somewhat like a turtle's. But as a rule it had an extremely long un-turtlelike neck and a small head. Its legs were paddles. The largest of these marine reptiles were 50 feet long, but most of them were not more than half that length. They were not fast swimmers but, with their long, sharp teeth, they were good hunters. The plesiosaurs did not become extinct until near the close of the Age of Reptiles, some 70 million years ago.

The name *ichthyosaur* means 'fish reptile.' As the picture shows, the name fits well. The ichthyosaurs were far bigger than most fishes of today. Some were 25 feet long or even longer. They were rapid swimmers and even though these fish reptiles seem to have been well fitted for living in the sea, all of them disappeared before the end of the Age of Reptiles.

The *mosasaurs* were ancient marine lizards. Fossils of them have been found in many different parts of the world. The biggest mosasaurs were from 30 to 40 feet long. They were perhaps the fiercest of the reptiles that lived in the sea. These marine lizards were common, late in the Age of Reptiles.

During the Age of Reptiles there were reptiles in the air as well as on land and in the water. The flying reptiles—the *pterosaurs* (winged reptiles), or *pterodactyls* (wing-fingers)—had big wings. *Pteranodon*, the last of the pterosaurs, had a wingspread of nearly 30 feet! Birds descended from the reptiles but not from the flying reptiles. The pterosaurs left no descendants to live on after the Age of Reptiles.

By far the best known of the reptiles that ruled the earth during the Age of Reptiles were the *dinosaurs*. The biggest dinosaurs were the largest animals that ever walked on land. The disappearance of the dinosaurs marked the end of the Age of Reptiles.

POISONOUS SNAKES

A great many people are afraid of snakes and think that any snake should be killed on sight. Actually most snakes are harmless, and some do a great deal of good by eating such animals as fieldmice and rats. There are, however, some poisonous snakes, and some are very harmful indeed. About 10,000 people die each year in India alone from the bites of poisonous snakes, and thousands more die in other tropical regions. Poisonous snakes inject their poison with fangs that are like hypodermic needles.

Deaths from snakebite have been cut down in recent years by the use of antivenins—antitoxins that work against the snake poisons. There are now few deaths from snakebite in Europe, the United States or Canada.
The ADDER is the best-known European snake—by name at least. It occurs in nearly all European countries and can grow to a length of 2½ feet. Its natural colour is grey, but there are many colour variations from red-brown to black. A typical distinguishing mark is the dark zig-zag band which is more or less visible down the whole length of its back.

Most of the poisonous snakes in the United States are RATTLESNAKES. There are rattlesnakes of one kind or another in almost every section of the country. The eastern diamond-back is the largest rattler and the United States' largest poisonous snake. It may be more than 8 feet long. Rattlesnakes get their name from the rattles on their tail. A rattlesnake often shakes its rattle when it is about to strike and thus gives a warning.

The COPPERHEAD gets its name from the coppery-brown colour of its head. This snake which is 3 to 4 feet long, is found chiefly in the south-eastern states of the U.S.A., but it may be found in every state east of the Mississippi River and in some of the southern states farther

WATER MOCCASIN

COMMON CORAL SNAKE

INDIAN COBRA

COPPERHEAD

EASTERN DIAMONDBACK

west. A copperhead fights very hard if it is trapped.

The WATER MOCCASIN, somewhat longer than the copperhead, is found in the south-eastern states. It lives in swampy regions. It belongs, as do also the copperhead and the rattlesnakes, to a group of poisonous snakes called pit vipers. They have pits between their eyes and their nostrils which, because they are sensitive to heat, help the snakes tell when they are near a warm-blooded animal. Another name for the water moccasin is 'cotton-mouth.' This name comes from the white lining of the snake's mouth.

CORAL SNAKES are beautifully coloured, but very poisonous. The common coral snake, which is about a yard long, is found in the south of the United States. The western coral snake is only about 1½ feet long. Coral snakes do not do as much harm as one would expect, for their fangs are too short to penetrate heavy cloth or shoe leather.

Of the poisonous snakes, the FER-DE-LANCE is one of the most dangerous. It is another of the pit vipers. This snake is found chiefly in the hot lands of northern South America. It may grow to be 8 feet long.

The fer-de-lance is a common snake, partly because a mother snake produces so many young—as many as 70 at a time. Within a few minutes from the time they are born the little snakes are able to defend themselves with their poison fangs

There are a dozen or so kinds of COBRAS. The Indian cobra can be blamed for a great many of the deaths from snakebite in India. The spreading heads, or hoods, of the cobras make them look quite different from most snakes. The Indian cobra, which is about 6 feet long, is the snake most often used by snake charmers. Kipling's famous story of Rikki-Tikki-Tavi is about an Indian cobra and a mongoose. Some of the cobras found in Africa can actually spit their poison for quite a distance and can blind an approaching enemy. A common way for a person in ancient Egypt to commit suicide was to let an asp—a kind of African cobra—bite him. The king cobra of Thailand is the largest of all poisonous snakes; it may be 18 feet long.

The TIGER SNAKE of Australia is a relative of the cobras. A full-grown tiger snake, which is about 6 feet long, has enough poison in its poison glands to kill 400 people. This snake, like the fer-de-lance, produces a great many young.

The MAMBA of Africa is another relative of the cobras. This snake may be 14 feet long. The natives of Africa are very much afraid of it. When a person comes close, it shows no disposition to run away, and its venom is deadly.

The GABOON VIPER of Africa belongs to the group of poisonous snakes called the true vipers. It is a huge snake; although it is no longer than the cobras, its body measures 6 inches across. The poison fangs of this big snake may be 1½ inches long. In the regions where it lives, however, this snake uses its poison almost entirely on animals it needs for food. Few Africans are actually bitten by it.

The TIC-POLONGA of south-eastern Asia is also one of the true vipers. Another name for it is Russell's viper. It is a somewhat smaller snake than the Indian cobra, but is almost as much feared. The tic-polonga would cause far fewer deaths if so many children did not go barefoot in the region where it lives.

TIGER SNAKE

ADDER

MAMBA

TIC-POLONGA

FER-DE-LANCE

GABOON VIPER

BIRDS

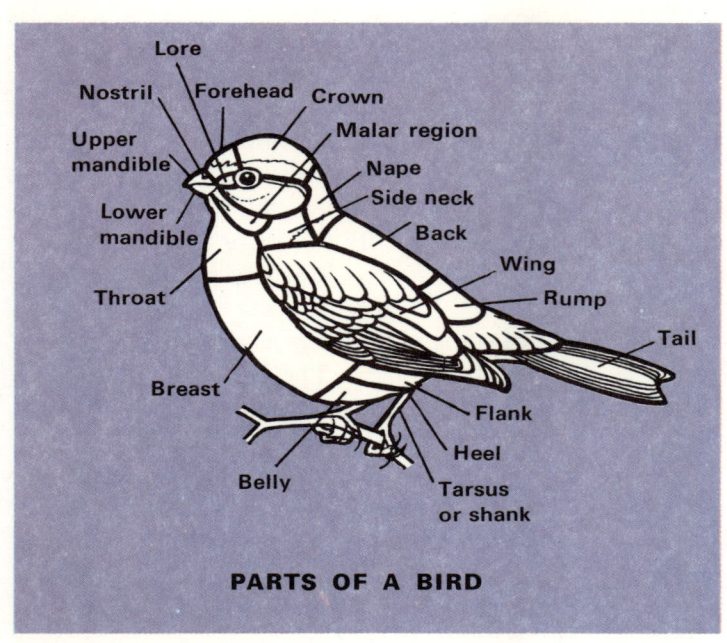

PARTS OF A BIRD

Birds are vertebrates; they all have backbones. Like mammals, they are warm-blooded. All birds have feathers when grown; and every animal with feathers is a bird.

Birds breathe with lungs all their lives.

All birds have two legs.

All birds have two wings, but in a few species the wings are so reduced in size that they are hidden and useless.

Although as a rule birds can fly, there are a number of species of flightless birds—e.g. the ostrich and penguin.

All birds hatch from eggs; there are no live-bearing birds.

Some birds when hatched are covered with down and can run about almost at once; others are naked and helpless.

A bird has a heart with four chambers, just as all mammals. No birds of today have teeth.

The normal temperature for a bird may be as high as 112°F.—a temperature that would be a terrifically high fever for a human being.

There are more than 20,000 species of birds. About 452 species are found in Europe.

Birds have been on earth for at least 150 million years.

THREE FLIGHTLESS GIANTS OF THE PAST

MOA

The tallest moas were about 11 feet tall—taller than any birds of today and any other birds of the past. The 'drumstick' of a moa giant was nearly a yard long. The moas lived in New Zealand. They disappeared some four centuries ago.

PHORORHACOS

Phororhacos lived in Patagonia some 20,000,000 years ago. It was about 6 feet tall and had an enormous head—one as big as the head of a horse. Its beak had a sharp hook, good for tearing meat.

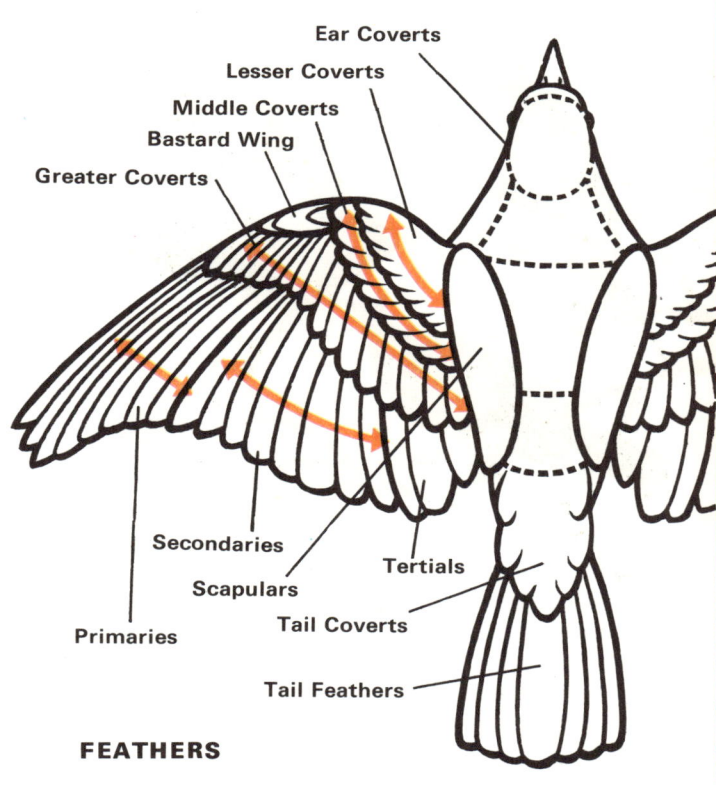

Ear Coverts
Lesser Coverts
Middle Coverts
Bastard Wing
Greater Coverts

Secondaries
Scapulars
Primaries
Tertials
Tail Coverts

Tail Feathers

FEATHERS

Aepyornis lived in Madagascar during the European Ice Age. This 'elephant bird' was as tall as an ostrich and laid much bigger eggs. They were more than a foot long, the biggest bird eggs anyone knows about.

AEPYORNIS

BIRD ORDERS

Flightless Birds Cassowaries, Emus, Kiwis, Ostriches, Rheas

Loons

Grebes

Petrels and Albatrosses

Penguins

Pelicans and Cormorants

Herons, Storks, Flamingos and Bitterns

Rails, Gallinules and Cranes

Gulls, Terns, Sandpipers, Auks and Plovers

Ducks, Geese and Swans

Grouse, Quail, Pheasants, Turkeys and Chickens

Vultures, Hawks and Eagles

Owls

Pigeons and Doves

Parrots

Cuckoos

Nightjars

Swifts and Hummingbirds

Kingfishers and Hornbills

Woodpeckers and Toucans

Perching Birds Blackbirds, Crows, Finches, Flycatchers, Grosbeaks, Jays, Magpies, Nuthatches, Robins, Sparrows, Swallows, Tanagers, Thrushes, Warblers, Wrens

GOLDCREST

YELLOWHAMMER

GREAT TIT

REDSTART

BLUE TIT

CHAFFINCH

BIRD FAMILIES

There are many thousand kinds of birds living today. They are to be found in all parts of the world. Each kind is specially adapted to take advantage of the place in which it lives. Many birds living near water have long legs so that they can wade through the shallows. Most of the water birds have webbed feet to help them to swim.

Although all birds have wings, not all of them can fly. The ostrich cannot fly. It uses its legs to race across the ground. The penguin is also too heavy for its wings to carry it up into the air. It can, however, use them as rudders when swimming.

The ostrich is the largest bird in the world today. In times past there were bigger ones. But compared with a humming bird, the ostrich is a giant. A fully grown male ostrich can weigh up to 300 lbs, whereas a humming bird weighs only 2 grammes (0.07 of an ounce).

Birds do not all feed in the same way. The shape of a bird's beak helps us to discover what kind of food it eats. Hawks and falcons have sharply curved beaks with which they can kill mice and other small mammals. Seed-eaters such as finches have broad, strong beaks with which to crack open seeds. Wrens have a sharp, narrow little beak with which they can peck insects out of the tiny cracks in tree bark. The beaks of humming birds are long and narrow so that they can plunge them down the narrow trumpet-shaped heads of flowers to collect the honey.

Birds also use their beaks to build their nests. Woodpeckers have such strong beaks that they can carve their nests out of the tough wood of a tree. A bird's beak performs functions similar to human hands. The nest of a swallow or a wren shows what wonderful 'hands' beaks can be.

Birds have feathers which are good protection against the weather. Feathers keep off the water because they are greasy and they are as warm as fur.

MALLARD

HOUSE SPARROW

GOLDEN ORIOLE
(COCK)

GOLDEN ORIOLE
(HEN)

LONG-EARED OWL

SPARROWHAWK

GREAT SPOTTED
WOODPECKER

BULLFINCH

SWALLOW

ROBIN

YELLOWHAMMER

NUTHATCH

ANIMAL RECORD HOLDERS

A pigmy goby is the smallest fish in the world and the smallest animal with a backbone. It is less than half an inch long.

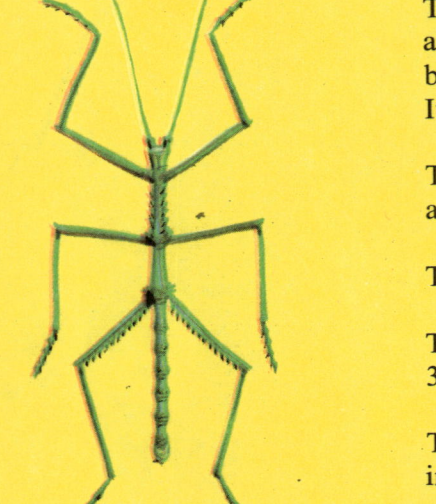

The blue whale is the largest animal in the world. So far as anyone knows, it is the largest animal that ever lived. It may be more than 90 feet long and weigh more than 100 tons. It is a mammal.

The stick insects are the longest of all insects. The longest are about 16 inches long.

The whale shark is the largest fish. It may be 45 feet long.

The anaconda is the longest and heaviest snake. It may be 35 feet long and weigh more than 250 pounds.

The Hercules moth of Australia has a wingspread of 14 inches and is the world's largest moth.

The African elephant is the largest land animal. It may weigh up to six tons. It is a mammal.

The true chameleon has the most amazing tongue found in the animal world. A seven-inch chameleon may have a twelve-inch tongue, which it can shoot out like lightning to catch an insect.

The giant tortoise is the longest-lived of all animals. It may live to be 150 years old.

FACTS ABOUT BRAINS

1 A full-grown person's brain weighs about 3 pounds.

2 A gorilla's brain weighs about $1\frac{1}{3}$ pounds.

3 An elephant has one pound of brain for every 1,000 pounds of body.

4 A blue whale weighs about 25 times as much as an elephant but its brain weighs only twice as much as an elephant's—about 20 pounds.

5 A dog's brain weighs about 6 ounces, a cat's about 1 ounce, and a horse's about 20 ounces.

6 The ordinary person weighs about 40 times as much as his brain.

7 A cod weighs about 5,000 times as much as its brain.

8 The brain of the 35-ton thunder lizard (Brontosaurus) weighed only about a pound. No wonder the dinosaurs disappeared from the earth!

9 The brain space in the skull of a person of today measures about 1,300 cubic centimeters. The brain space in the skull of the Java ape man (Pithecanthropus erectus) measured about 900 cubic centimeters.

The ostrich is the largest bird. It may be eight feet tall and weigh 200 pounds.

The peregrine falcon, or duck hawk, is the fastest flier. It can fly three miles a minute.

The arctic tern takes the longest trips on its own power of any animal. An arctic tern may travel more than 20,000 miles in a single year.

The giant salamander of Japan is the largest amphibian. It may be five feet long.

The smallest shrews are the smallest of all mammals. A full-grown one weighs only about an ounce.

The albatross has a greater wingspread than any other bird. It may measure seven feet.

The hummingbirds are the smallest birds. A full-grown ruby-throated hummingbird weighs less than an ounce.

The giraffe is the tallest animal. It may be 19 feet tall.

The largest animal without a backbone is the giant squid. A giant squid may be more than 50 feet long.

The cheetah can run faster than any other animal. It can run at speeds of up to 60 m.p.h. over short distances.

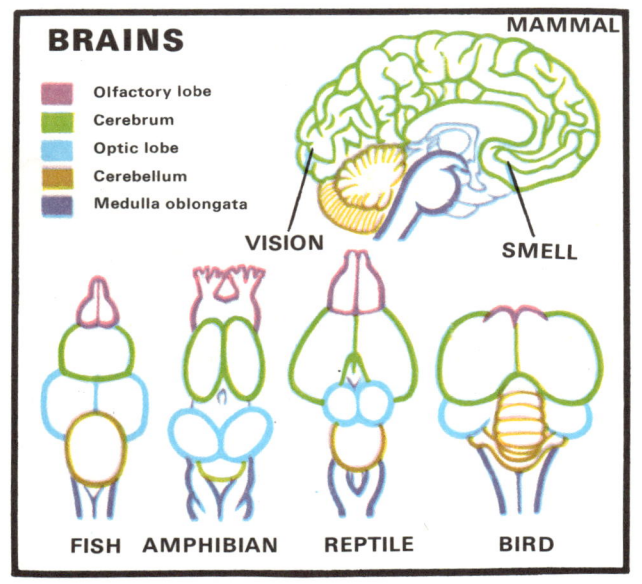

BRAINS

- Olfactory lobe
- Cerebrum
- Optic lobe
- Cerebellum
- Medulla oblongata

VISION   SMELL   MAMMAL

FISH   AMPHIBIAN   REPTILE   BIRD

TEN OF THE MOST INTELLIGENT ANIMALS

CHIMPANZEE   ORANG-UTAN   GORILLA   MONKEY   DOG

CAT   RACCOON   ELEPHANT   PIG   HORSE

DID YOU KNOW?

Every termite nest has its king and queen. All the other termites in the nest—there may be millions—are their children.

Petrels get their name from Peter, one of the Twelve Apostles, who, according to the story in the New Testament, walked to Jesus on the waves of a storm-tossed lake. Petrels often hover close to the surface of the sea with their feet actually in the water and look as if they are walking on the waves.

Hummingbirds can fly backwards.

Some animals can grow, or regenerate, lost parts. A lobster that loses a claw can grow a new one. If a little flat-worm is cut in two cross-ways, its head-half will grow a new tail, and its tail-half will grow a new head.

The duckbilled platypus is the only mammal that has poison glands.

Army ants, when they stop for a few days at a time on their marches, build nests out of their own bodies for their queen and for the larvae and pupae. When the stay is over, the ants forming the walls of a nest separate and are ready to march again.

Some crabs camouflage themselves by 'planting' small animals such as sponges, sea anemones, and hedgehog hydroids on their backs. These animals stay where they are put.

Some kinds of ants and termites are farmers. They raise fungus gardens.

Ants and termites may have their own variety of 'domes-ticated' animals which they keep in their nests. These domesticated animals are other insects such as aphids, tree-hoppers, and beetles.

Seals, although they spend most of their lives in water, are always born on land and, as babies, have to be taught to swim.

The alligator is the only reptile with a loud voice. Its bellow can be heard a mile away.

The pika, or little chief hare, cuts hay during the summer, dries it in the sun, and stores it in cracks in rocks. In the winter the animal lives on food from its 'hayloft.'

A cricket can be used as a thermometer, because the number of times it chirps per minute varies with the tem-perature. At a temperature a little above freezing, it chirps

NINE ANIMALS THAT HAVE BECOME EXTINCT IN MODERN TIMES

PASSENGER PIGEON

The last passenger pigeon anyone knows about died 1 September, 1914, in a zoo in Cincinnati. A hundred and fifty years ago the passenger pigeon was so common that the size of the flocks was one of the wonders of the bird world. But much killing and the cutting down of the forests where the bird nested caused it to disappear.

ESKIMO CURLEW

In the autumn Eskimo curlews used to fly southward from Newfoundland in such millions that they darkened the sky. They were killed by the hundreds of thousands for food. Since 1900 no live birds have been seen.

WEST INDIAN SEAL

This seal was much hunted during colonial days and has not been seen at all since 1912.

QUAGGA

The quagga has been extinct since about 1880. It too, was hunted so much that it could not survive. It was once very common on the grassy plains of Africa.

STELLER'S SEA COW

This sea cow was a relative of the manatee but was much larger. It was first discovered near Alaska about 1740 and was killed off in less than thirty years.

 TREE SLOTH

 MOLE

 RAT

47 times a minute, and at 70° F., 150 times a minute.

The tree sloth has four legs, but it never walks on them. Instead, it hangs by them from the branches of trees.

A mole 6 inches long has been known to dig a tunnel 100 yards long in a single night.

The water ouzel, a bird of the Rocky Mountains, often builds its nest behind a waterfall.

Paper wasps were making paper out of wood many thousands of years before people learned to do so.

The kiwi, a bird of New Zealand, has only small remnants of wings, which are completely hidden by feathers.

The jellyfish called the Portuguese man-of-war is not a single animal but a whole colony of small animals.

A young bird may eat more than its weight in food in a single day.

A worker honeybee dies when it stings an enemy, for it cannot pull out its sting. It tears its body to pieces trying to do so.

One pair of Norway rats could have 350 million descendants in only three years. There are, as a rule, ten litters a year with ten young in each litter.

A big sponge may furnish shelter for thousands of smaller animals. More than 17,000, among them some fishes, were counted in a sponge a yard across found near Florida.

In every flock of hens a pecking order is established. Every hen except the lowest one in the pecking order can peck certain hens, and every one except the one at the top can be pecked by others. The higher a hen is in the pecking order, the better chance it has to get all the food it wants and a good roosting place.

Austria's famous white performing horses, the Lippizaners, are dark when they are colts. They do not get their white coats until they are at least three years old.

Honeybees tell their fellow workers by different kinds of dances where nectar and pollen can be found.

One of the most ingenious devices in nature is the silken door a trap-door spider builds to close the entrance to its nest.

Many people consider the Cape buffalo the most dangerous of all animals. More hunters have been killed by it than by any other big game animal.

GREAT AUK
The great auk has been extinct since about 1844. This bird, once very common on islands near the eastern coast of North America, was killed off by hunters who wanted its meat for food and its feathers for featherbeds.

CALIFORNIAN GRIZZLY BEAR
There are not even any mounted specimens of this very big bear in museums. Early settlers in the western U.S.A. killed it because they were afraid of it.

DODO
The dodo once was common on two islands in the Indian Ocean. But it has been extinct since 1681. When the sailors who landed on the islands came near dodoes, the birds did not try to escape. They could not fly, but they did not even walk away. 'As dead as a dodo' came to be a common saying. Sailors, hogs, and monkeys killed the dodo off.

LABRADOR DUCK
The last known Labrador duck was killed near Long Island (N.Y.) in 1875. No one knows very much about this bird—where it nested or exactly where it spent the winters. Probably hunters killed it chiefly for its feathers. At any rate, the only Labrador ducks of today are about forty stuffed specimens in museums.

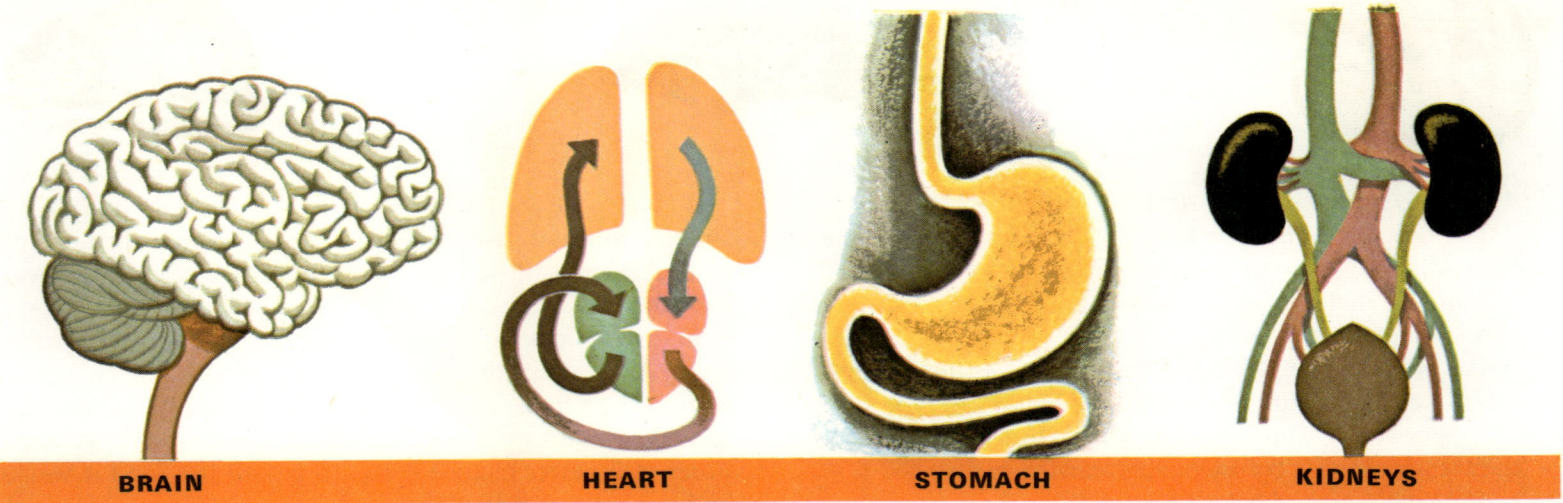

| BRAIN | HEART | STOMACH | KIDNEYS |

BODY SYSTEMS

SYSTEMS	PURPOSES SERVED	MADE UP OF
SKELETAL	Forms a framework for the body.	Bones and ligaments.
MUSCULAR	Brings about all body movements.	Muscles and tendons.
CIRCULATORY	Carries food and oxygen to all parts of the body and carries wastes away.	Heart, arteries, veins, capillaries and blood.
DIGESTIVE	Digests food—turns it into a liquid—so that it can enter tne blood, and gets rid of food wastes.	Mouth, teeth, throat, œsophagus, stomach, liver, gall-bladder, pancreas, small intestine and large intestine.
RESPIRATORY	Takes in oxygen and gets rid of carbon dioxide	Nose, throat, windpipe, bronchial tubes and lungs.
NERVOUS	Acts as the body's engineer, lets a person know what is going on about him, and makes it possible to solve problems and to think.	Brain, spinal cord and nerves.
ENDOCRINE	Produces hormones and by means of them controls some body activities.	Glands such as the pituitary, thyroid, parathyroids, adrenals and islands of Langerhans.
URINARY	Removes wastes from blood and washes them from the body in urine.	Kidneys, ureters, bladder and urethra.
LYMPHATIC	Keeps the cells of the body bathed in fluid, and passes food to the cells from the blood.	Lymph vessels, lymph glands and lymph.
REPRODUCTIVE	Produces children.	Ovaries and uterus (female); testes (male).
SENSORY	Relays information about the outside world to the nervous system.	Skin, eyes, nose, tongue and ears.

IN ONE DAY

If an adult is of average weight and in good health, in every 24 hours:
His heart beats about 100,000 times.
His heart pumps about 1,800 gallons of blood.
He breathes about 23,000 times.
He breathes in about 400 cubic feet of air.
He takes out of the air about 20 cubic feet of oxygen.
He eats about 3 pounds of food.
He drinks about $2\frac{1}{2}$ pints of liquid.
He loses in perspiration about $1\frac{1}{3}$ pints of water.
He produces 2 to 3 pints of saliva.
His nails grow about .000046 of an inch.
His hair grows about .01714 of an inch.
He speaks about 5,000 words.

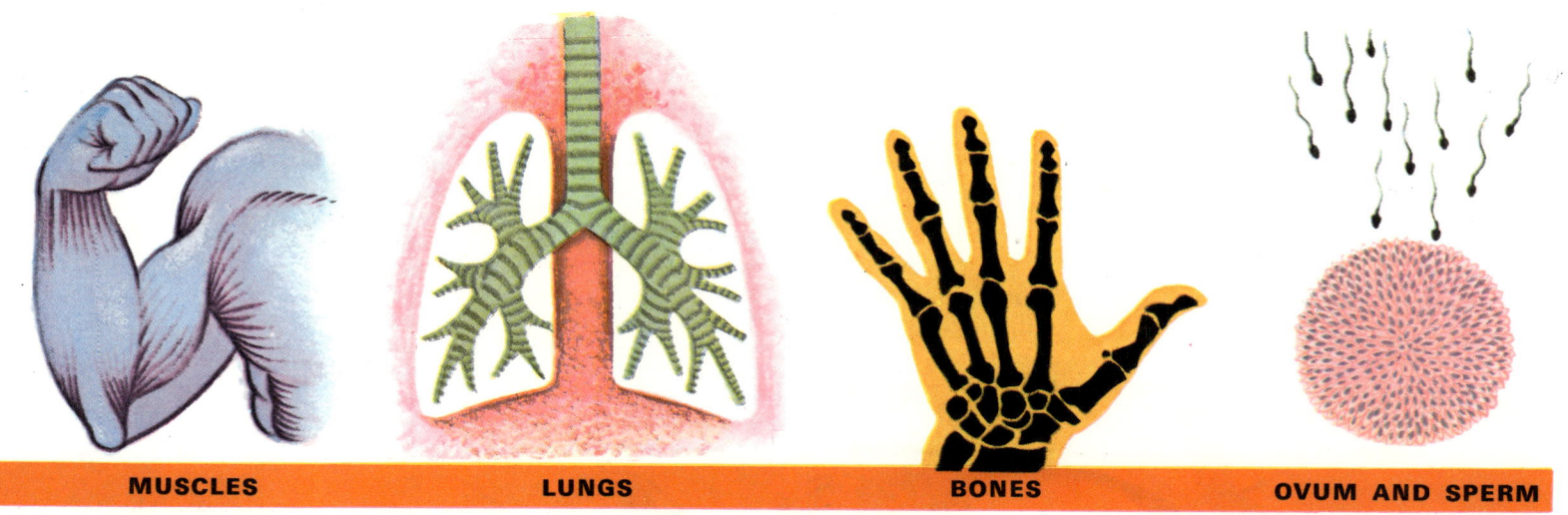

MUSCLES   LUNGS   BONES   OVUM AND SPERM

MORE FIGURES

The normal skeleton is made up of 209 bones; a child has more, but some of them fuse together as he grows up.

More than half the number of bones—108 to be exact—are in wrists, ankles, hands and feet.

The body contains $\frac{1}{2}$ ounce of sugar, 1 ounce of salt, $3\frac{1}{2}$ pounds of calcium, enough iron to make one nail, enough carbon for the leads of 9,000 pencils, enough phosphorus for the heads of 2,000 matches and enough fat for 7 bars of soap.

A grown person's brain weighs nearly 3 pounds. The wrinkled, grey covering layer of the brain is made up of more than 9,000,000,000 cells.

Messages travel along our nerves at speeds ranging from 1-300 feet a second.

There are more than 600 muscles in the muscular system.

A person has two sets of teeth. There are 20 teeth in the first milk set; there are 32 in the second, or permanent, set.

Water accounts for about $\frac{2}{3}$ of the weight of the body.

The stomach can be stretched to hold approximately a quart of liquid.

A person's small intestine is from 3 to 4 times as long as he is tall. His large intestine is only 4 or 5 feet long.

The temperature marked 'normal' on a fever thermometer is 98.6°F. The temperature of a healthy person is usually between 98°F. and 99°F. In a fever the temperature may rise to 110°F.

There are millions of tiny air sacs in the lungs. Their total inside surface is about 100 square yards.

A person normally breathes from 16 to 18 times a minute; the rate goes down during sleep and up during strenuous exercise.

The lungs can hold from 5 to 8 pints of air. About a pint is taken in at each breath.

A man's heart weighs 11 or 12 ounces, a woman's 8 or 9.

An adult weighing 150 pounds has about 9-10 pints of blood.

All the blood vessels of a person's body, if laid end to end, would reach 100,000 miles.

Blood takes only about one minute to leave the heart, circle the body, and get back to the heart again.

The normal pulse rate for an adult is from 60 to 80 beats a minute, with 70 the average while at rest.

In a person weighing 100 pounds there are about 25 billion red blood cells and only 35,000 million white cells.

Red blood cells live about 127 days. In a single hour about 8,000 million are destroyed and replaced.

Red cells are so small that it would take thousands to make a pile 1 inch high.

The kidneys filter about 170 quarts of fluid a day to remove wastes. Most of the fluid they filter returns to the blood.

The complete skin covering of the body measures about 20 square feet.

In the skin of the palms of the hands there may be as many as 3,000 sweat glands to the square inch.

A person has from 90,000 to 140,000 hairs on his head. Red-haired people, as a rule, have fewer hairs than brunettes or blondes.

OUR SENSES

SEEING

The eye is very much like a camera. It has a lens just as a camera has. The eye's lens is better than a camera lens because it can change its shape to focus the image of both far and near objects on the retina. The retina is like the film of the camera. The iris, which can change the size of the opening for light—the pupil—is like the diaphragm of the camera.

The eyeball is kept moist and clean by blinking. The average person blinks his eyes 25 times a minute. Each blink lasts about $\frac{1}{5}$ of a second.

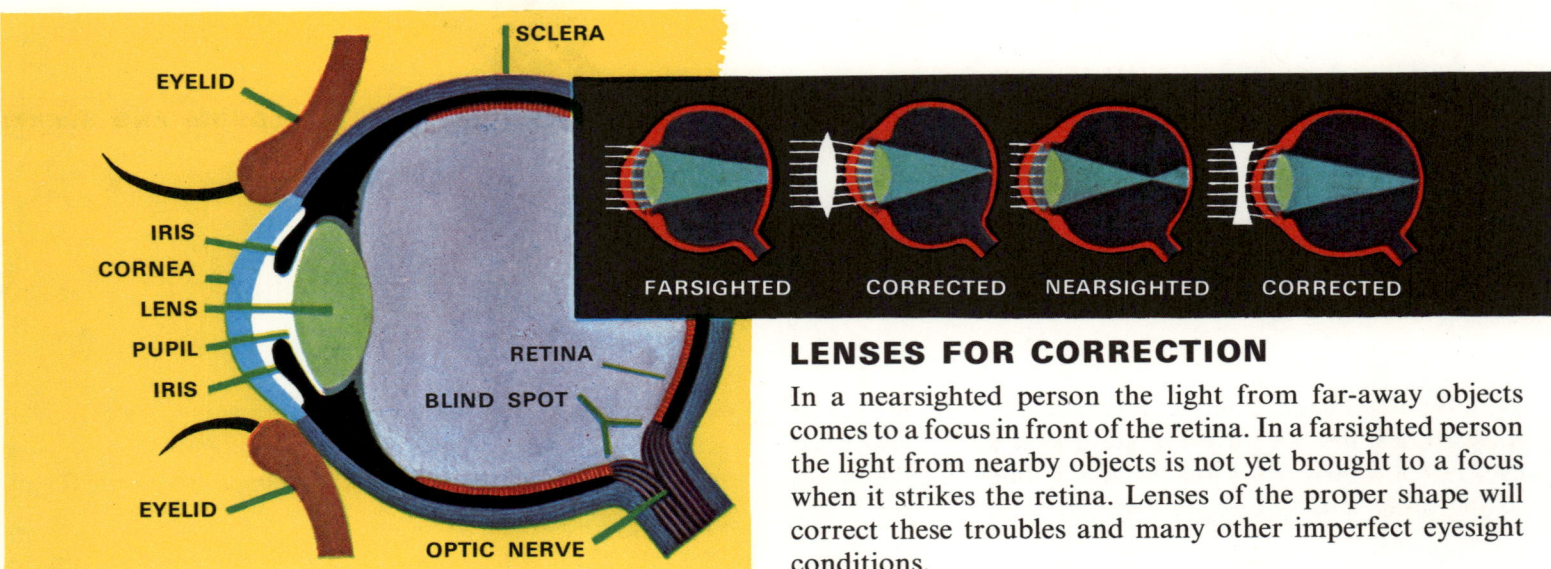

SCLERA
EYELID
IRIS
CORNEA
LENS
PUPIL
IRIS
EYELID
RETINA
BLIND SPOT
OPTIC NERVE

FARSIGHTED   CORRECTED   NEARSIGHTED   CORRECTED

LENSES FOR CORRECTION

In a nearsighted person the light from far-away objects comes to a focus in front of the retina. In a farsighted person the light from nearby objects is not yet brought to a focus when it strikes the retina. Lenses of the proper shape will correct these troubles and many other imperfect eyesight conditions.

HEARING

The nerves of hearing end in the cochlea of the inner ear. Sound waves strike the eardrum and make it vibrate. Little bones in the middle ear carry the vibrations to the liquid which fills the inner ear. The vibrations of this fluid affect the nerves that carry sound messages to the brain.

The semi-circular canals which are a part of the inner ear are very important in helping a person keep his balance.

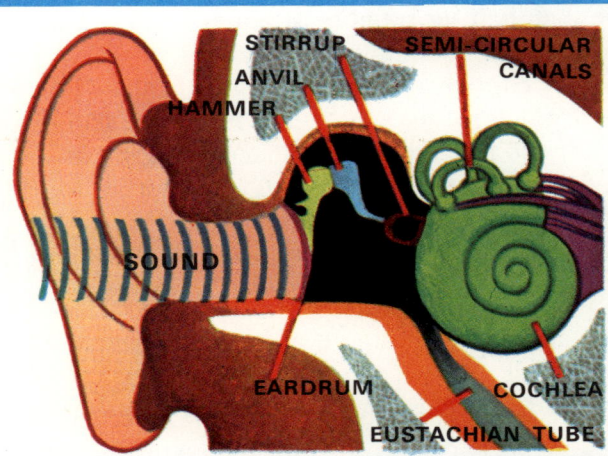

STIRRUP   SEMI-CIRCULAR
ANVIL   CANALS
HAMMER
SOUND
EARDRUM   COCHLEA
EUSTACHIAN TUBE

FEELING

Different nerves of touch carry different messages, such as heat, cold, pain, touch and pressure. In the skin alone there are 45 miles of nerves. Nerve endings are so close together in some areas of skin that pressure points with only $\frac{1}{25}$ of an inch between them can be told apart.

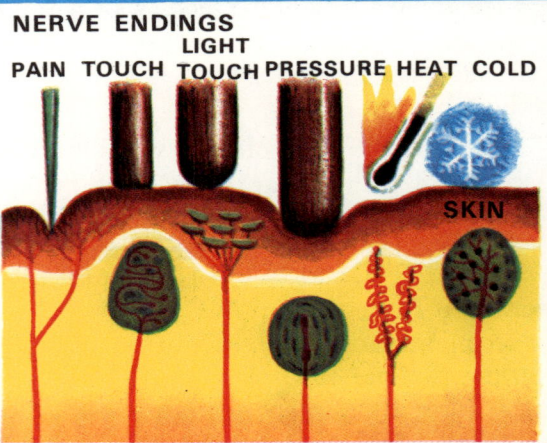

NERVE ENDINGS
LIGHT
PAIN TOUCH TOUCH PRESSURE HEAT COLD
SKIN

EYE BALANCE

Stand a 3 in. by 5 in. card on one of its longer edges on the line between the fishbowl and the fish. Bend down until your nose touches the card. One of your eyes now sees the fishbowl and the other the fish. Remain in this position for a minute or so, concentrating on the picture and remembering to keep both eyes open. Eventually your brain will fuse the two pictures if your eyes have the proper balance, and you will see the fish swim into the bowl.

BLIND SPOT

On the retina of each eye there is a blind spot, the place where tiny nerves of the retina unite to form the optic nerve. To show yourself that there is a blind spot, do this: hold this page at arm's length. Close your left eye and look with your right eye at the cross below. You will be able to see the red dot, too. If you move the page towards you, the dot will disappear when the light reflected from it strikes the blind spot.

EYE TEST

With both eyes open, point with your finger to some spot on the wall or ceiling of the room you are in. Close your right eye. Do not move your finger. Is your finger still pointing to the same spot? Close your left eye. Is your finger still pointing to that spot? If your finger appears to have moved when you close your right eye, you are right-eyed. If your finger appears to have moved when you close your left eye, you are left-eyed.

TASTING

In the tongue there are taste buds in which there are the endings of nerves of taste. There are buds of four kinds, giving us four taste sensations: sweet, sour, bitter and salty. All other tastes are really smells. The sweet and salty taste buds are at the front of the tongue, the sour buds along the sides, and the bitter at the back. There are no taste buds in the middle of the tongue. A person has about 3,000 taste buds. It takes a person about a third of a second to taste something salty and a whole second to taste something bitter.

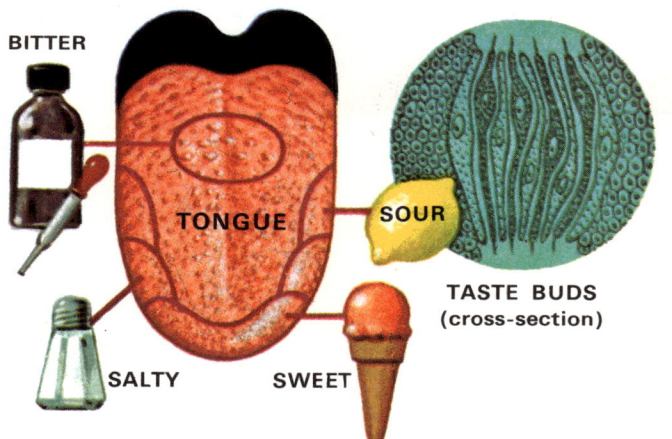

SMELLING

All the endings of the nerves of smell are in the linings of the nose passages. Most of what we call taste is really smell. When nerves of smell are kept from doing their work by a cold or dryness, by some permanent injury or smoking cigarettes excessively, most foods taste alike.

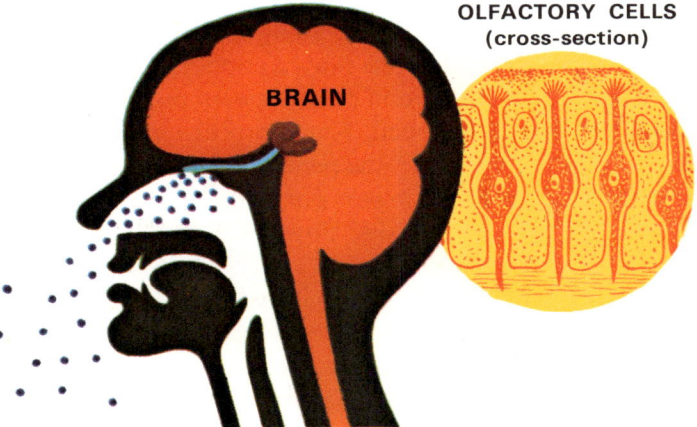

OPTICAL ILLUSIONS

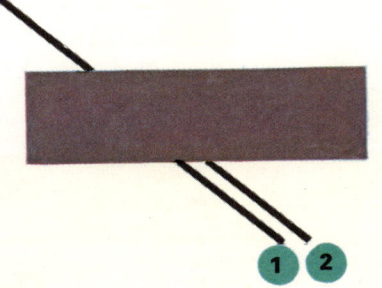

Is the line above the rectangle a continuation of 1 or 2?

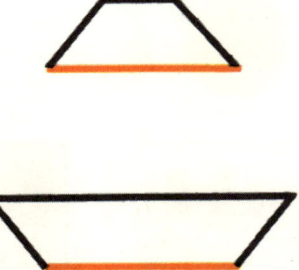

Are the red lines in these two figures the same length?

Is this hat as tall as it is wide?

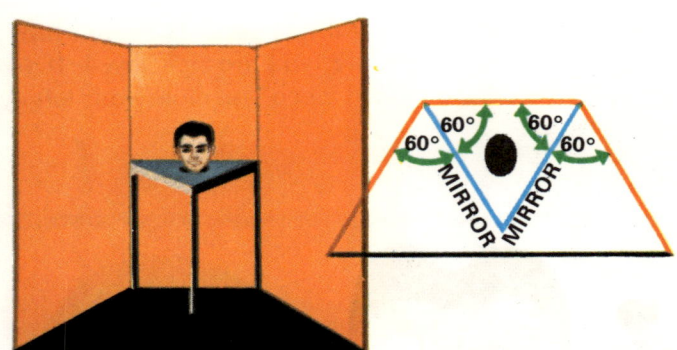

A SIMPLE MAGICIAN'S TRICK

In this trick a head appears to have no body. The optical illusion is brought about with mirrors. As a result of having the walls and mirrors at exactly the right angles, the walls and floor reflected in the mirrors appear to be the wall back of the table and the floor under it. Actually the man's body is hidden by the mirrors.

MOVING PICTURES

Divide two 3 in. by 5 in. cards in half as shown in the illustration. On the upper half of one draw a copper flower bowl. On the upper half of the second card draw an outline of the same bowl very lightly in pencil. Then draw bright-coloured flowers to fill it. Now rub out the pencil outline; it is meant only to help you place the flowers correctly.

Turn one of the cards upside down. Put the two cards back to back and fasten them with a rubber band to a straight rod or pencil. Hold the rod or pencil by the ends and twirl the cards. You should see the flowers in the bowl. Your eyes hold any picture they see for a short time. When the cards are twirled fast, your eyes see both pictures at the same time.

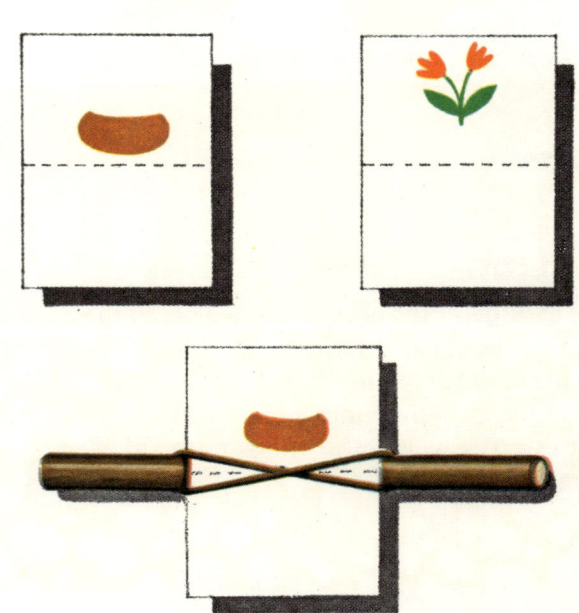

The two frames are perfect squares.

The two centre circles have exactly the same diameter.

The centre rectangles are equally dark.

CAMOUFLAGE

Colours and colour patterns help to protect many animals. Some animals change colour when their surroundings change.

During the World Wars much was done with colour and colour patterns to camouflage troops, warships, aircraft, tanks and military installations of various kinds. By the end of World War II, however, infra-red photographs taken from aircraft were 'seeing through' camouflage paint and making camouflage much more difficult.

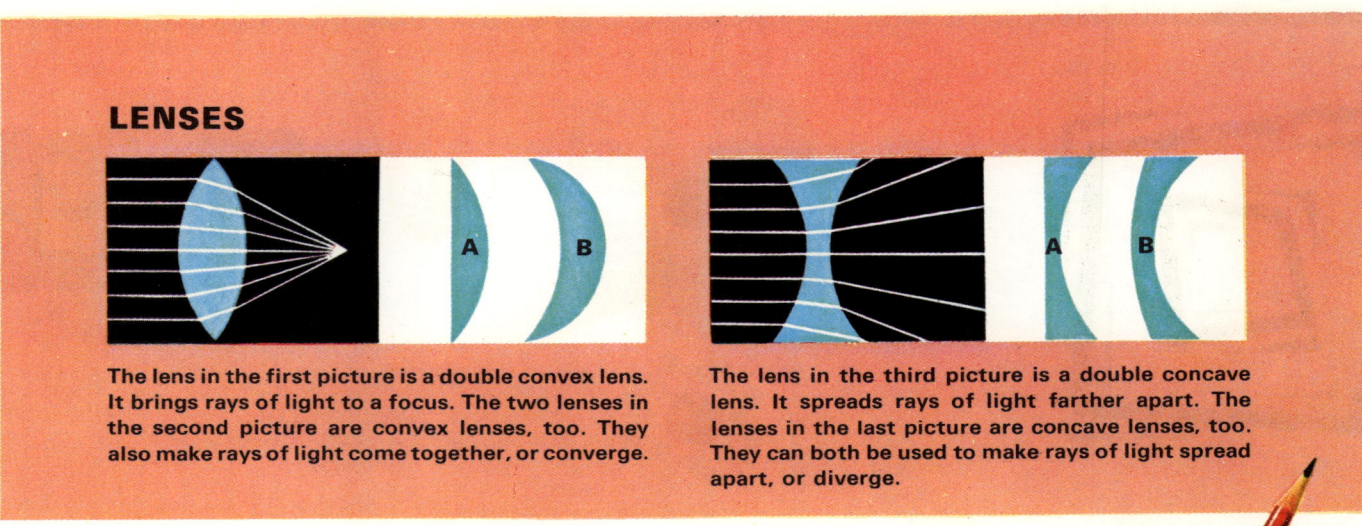

LENSES

The lens in the first picture is a double convex lens. It brings rays of light to a focus. The two lenses in the second picture are convex lenses, too. They also make rays of light come together, or converge.

The lens in the third picture is a double concave lens. It spreads rays of light farther apart. The lenses in the last picture are concave lenses, too. They can both be used to make rays of light spread apart, or diverge.

TWO EXPERIMENTS WITH REFRACTION

Put a small, shallow metal or opaque plastic bowl on a table. Place a coin on the bottom of the bowl. Move the bowl away from you slowly until the far edge of the coin is just out of sight. Then ask someone to pour water into the bowl. The coin will come into view.

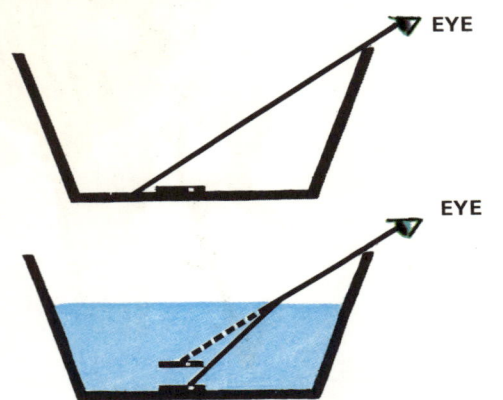

The light reflected from the coin is bent as it goes at a slant from the water into the air. When the coin comes into view after water has been poured into the bowl you are seeing it not where it really is but in the direction from which the light enters your eye.

Stand a pencil in a glass two-thirds full of water so that it rests against the top edge. The bending of the rays of light as they pass through the water into the air not only makes the pencil appear to be broken at the surface of the water but also makes the part of the pencil in the water appear to be bigger than it is. The curve of the side of the glass makes the water into a magnifying glass.

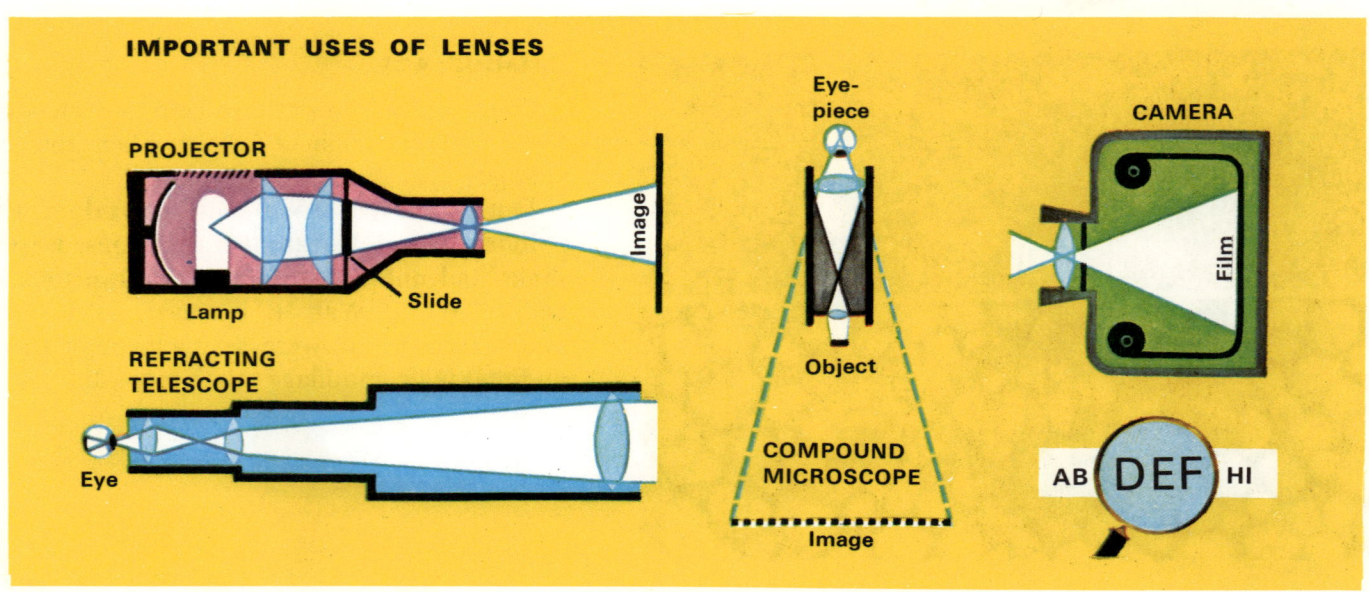

IMPORTANT USES OF LENSES

THE SPECTRUM

With a prism sunlight can be broken up into the colours of which it is made. The colours are violet, indigo, blue, green, yellow, orange and red.

DOUBLE RAINBOW

A rainbow is formed when droplets of water in the air act as prisms. Sometimes there is a double rainbow. In the two rainbows of a double rainbow the colours, as the diagram shows, are reversed.

WHY A RED ROSE IS RED

The petals of a red rose absorb all the colours except red. They reflect the red rays to our eyes, and the rose therefore looks red.

AFTER-IMAGE

Stare at the red birds while you count to 30. Then look up quickly to the ceiling of the room you are in. You should see blue-green birds there. If the ceiling is too dark for the birds to show, look at a sheet of white paper instead.

When you stare at the birds your eyes become too tired of red to see it any longer. When you look at the ceiling you still see the birds for a very short time, but you see them as blue-green. If the birds in the picture were blue, you would see them as brownish-yellow when you looked up at the ceiling.

A DISAPPEARING CAGE

Lay a piece of bright red cellophane over this picture. The cage disappears, and the parrot is free to fly away.

The red cellophane allows only red and orange rays to pass through it. The red-orange rays from the cage are lost in the red-orange rays reflected from the white background. The cage therefore disappears. At the same time, since no blue rays or green rays can go through the cellophane, the parrot is now all red and black.

BRITISH DECIMAL CURRENCY

The decimal system, like the old pound-shilling-pence (£-s-d) system, is based on the pound sterling. But since 15 February 1971—Decimal Day—the pound has been divided into 100 new pence, instead of 20 shillings each worth 12 pence.

In the past, we used three units to measure money values: the pound, the shilling and the penny.

In decimal currency there are only two units to measure money: the pound and the new penny.

Six new coins have been introduced which replace the old ten shilling note, the halfpenny, penny, shilling, florin and halfcrown.

The symbol for the pound in decimal currency is £ and the abbreviation for the new penny is p.

A decimal point is used to write amounts in pounds and pence. For example:

OLD SYSTEM	DECIMAL SYSTEM	HAND WRITTEN
£275	£275.00	Two hundred and seventy-five pounds—00
£5	£5.00	Five pounds—00
£5/10/0	£5.50	Five pounds—50

Design for the obverse side of all decimal coins.

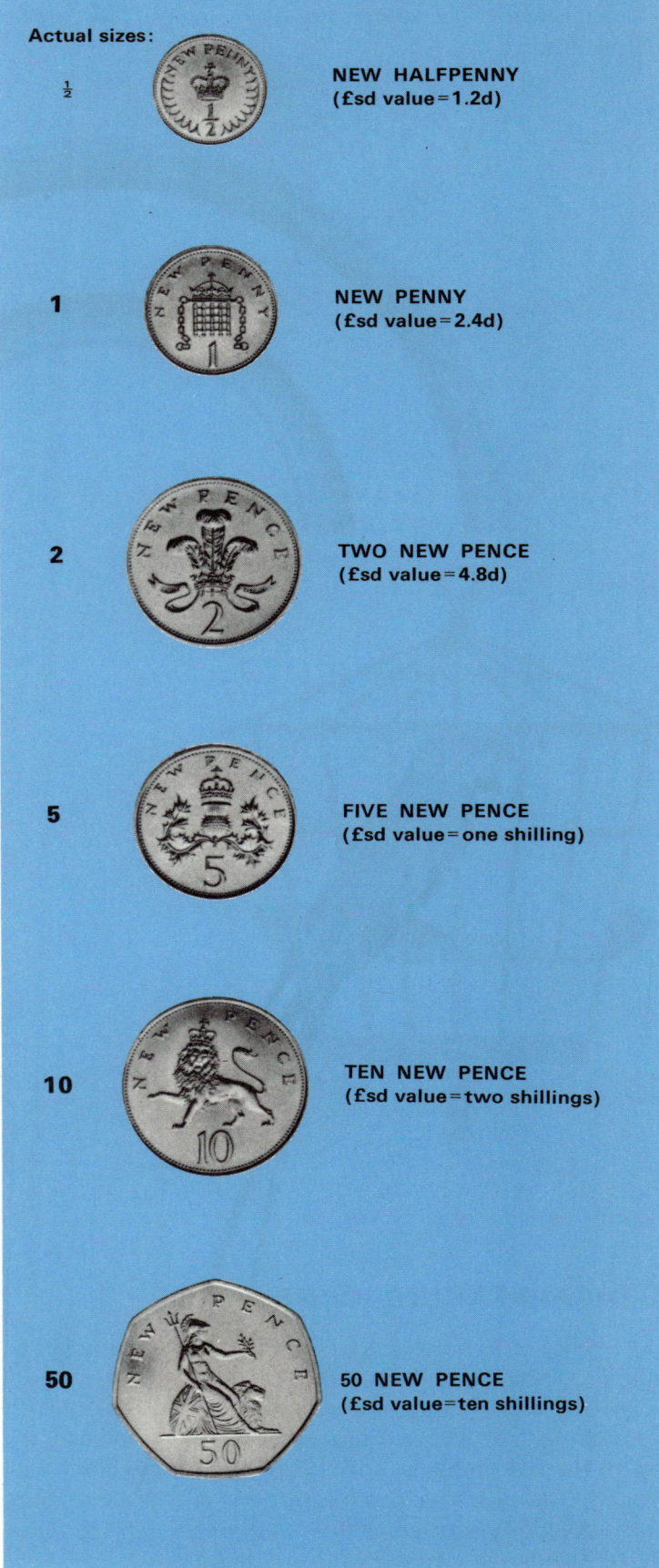

Actual sizes:

½ — NEW HALFPENNY (£sd value = 1.2d)

1 — NEW PENNY (£sd value = 2.4d)

2 — TWO NEW PENCE (£sd value = 4.8d)

5 — FIVE NEW PENCE (£sd value = one shilling)

10 — TEN NEW PENCE (£sd value = two shillings)

50 — 50 NEW PENCE (£sd value = ten shillings)

INDEX